SENIOR MANUAL FOR
GROUP LEADERSHIP

SENIOR MANUAL FOR GROUP LEADERSHIP

AN INSTANT USE GUIDE TO PARLIAMENTARY PROCEDURE WITH LESSONS

BY

O. GARFIELD JONES

PROFESSOR OF POLITICAL SCIENCE IN THE
UNIVERSITY OF THE CITY OF TOLEDO

NEW YORK
D. APPLETON-CENTURY COMPANY
INCORPORATED

TO MY WIFE
NELLIE NIXON JONES

Preface

The purpose of these lessons is to facilitate learning the art, the technique, of democratic self-government in high school and college groups and in adult groups generally.

Democracy, government by public opinion, representative government are under fire these days. In desperation many nations have gone back to the dictator government from which we emerged so painfully but gloriously only a few centuries ago. Perhaps it might be said of democracy (in these dictator countries) what Chesterton said of Christianity during the World War:—"It has not been 'tried and found wanting'. Rather has it been found hard and never tried."

Some centures ago rural England gave to the world the system of representative government and evolved the technique for operating it. Furthermore, the British people adapted this technique to urban conditions during the nineteenth century. The English also transplanted this system and this technique to rural America. It is our problem in the twentieth century (with the help of all the people within our borders) to adapt this system and this technique to the urban civilization which we have evolved to date.

One great problem of democracy is that of developing competent leaders. But leadership is not **a thing** to be constructed from inanimate matter,   rather is it a social product that results from the inter action of the individual with the group. The individual leader must have certain fundamental abilities it is true, but it is equally true that this individual must learn to exercise these abilities in such a harmonious relation to the group that the group **can** follow and **will** follow. And this harmonious relationship depends quite as much upon the desires, prejudices and abilities of the group as upon the desires, prejudices and abilities of the individual leader.

The best system of rules for the conduct of group discussion and action is called parliamentary procedure because this system of rules was evolved by the British Parliament during its centuries of experience in operating the government of Great Britain. These rules were slightly modified by the Congress of the United States into our congressional procedure. Then in 1876 General Henry M. Robert simplified these rules so as to adapt them to the use of ordinary societies and got this "adaptation" accepted generally throughout the United States as the standard "rules of order" for group meetings.

The technique required to preside over a group meeting or to lead the fight for or against any proposed group action I call "group leadership".

The great need, as I see it, is not for a large number of technical parliamentarians. On the contrary, the great need is for such a general diffusion of knowledge of the simpler rules of parliamentary procedure and for such a wide-spread emotional training for group leadership that our many, many clubs, societies and civic organizations will be conducted efficiently, intelligently, and in accordance with the expressed will of the majority after the minority have been given a fair hearing.

If democracy is to continue we must teach the technique of democratic citizenship, the art of citizen participation in the government of his own affairs. If representative government is to survive this generation in this most complicated industrial society we must teach representative government instead of merely teaching **about it.** Government of the people, by the people, and for the people is possible only when the people are making a daily practice of self-government in some form.

These lessons are designed to teach the art of self-government on a democratic basis in the hope that high school and college students and adults generally will use this technique in governing their own group affairs.

Self-governing ability is a technique, a habit of conduct, and an attitude of mind to the effect that the ordinary citizen can be, should be and will be effective in government. These lessons are designed to teach this technique. The use of this technique should be encouraged until it becomes a political habit. And out of this habit, together with emotional transfer from the inspiring teacher to the developing student, should come the attitude of mind that this student can be, should be, and will be effective as a citizen working for good government the remainder of his (or her) life.

These lessons for teaching parliamentary procedure and group leadership are the product of fourteen years experience in teaching some three thousand students. Messrs. Virgil Sheppard, J. Otis Garber, H. T. Shenefield, Orville R. Altman, Donovan F. Emch, and Charles F. Carson have contributed to the evolution of this teaching technique while conducting classes by this system. Mr. Lehr Fess, sometime Parliamentarian of the United States House of Representatives, has contributed much in the way of advice as to technical procedure both as teacher of Congressional Procedure in my department one year and as personal consultant on difficult points.

Dean Raymond L. Carter and Dr. Jesse L. Ward gave many suggestions and criticisms that materially improved the technical pedagogy of the lessons. I am also indebted to the students in my classes on "teaching group leadership", especially to Miss Irene O'Brien, who contributed much to the adaptation of this technique to public school use.

O. Garfield Jones.

Note for Teachers:—The best teaching is always a happy combination of intelligence and emotional transfer. The group leadership teacher who is all inspiration may ignore the rules of procedure and thus teach the students to be intellectual anarchists. The group leadership teacher who is all intellect may teach the students to be so technical as to paralyze group discussion and action. A "procedurette" is a person who makes his or her knowledge a means of "showing off" technical skill as an end in itself.

The best teacher of group leadership treats parliamentary procedure only as a means to achieve the desired end of group efficiency. This teacher inspires the students to have a great urge for making their group effective in a good cause. Good citizenship means nothing more than being effective in a good cause. And in an urban civilization effectiveness must be achieved through groups.

O. G. J.

Table of Contents

Note:—All page references in the lessons refer to the Senior Manual ("Parliamentary Procedure at a Glance").

SENIOR LESSONS IN GROUP LEADERSHIP

TRAINING IN CITIZENSHIP

Good citizenship is not a set of rules or a collection of facts. It is a habit of conduct, a way of living. The good citizen gives his best thoughts and efforts to the service of the community, the city, the state and the nation.

However, this does not mean that the good citizen forces his own ideas on the other members of the community. On the contrary, it means in the long run, majority rule. This is to say that the good citizen gives his best thoughts and efforts to the community, but when the majority of the community reject his ideas and adopt other ideas, this good citizen accepts the decision of the majority and obeys that decision until the community is persuaded to change that decision.

This principle of majority rule immediately raises the question as to how the community (the group) arrives at its majority decisions. The answer to this question in the United States is easy because it so happens that the English and American people have had over a thousand years of uninterrupted experience in self-government. This experience has taught us two things. The first is that the best way to arrive at a majority opinion in a very large group of thousands or millions of people is by a secret ballot.

The other thing that we have learned is that in smaller groups of less than a thousand (usually less than a hundred) the best way to arrive at a majority opinion is by making a specific motion, by amending that motion, discussing it thoroughly and then voting on it according to the rules for a deliberative assembly which we have worked out in this thousand years of self-government experience. These rules for the conduct of a deliberative assembly are called "Parliamentary Law" or "Rules of Parliamentary Procedure," or, in America, "Rules of Order" since they are the rules by which order is maintained while freedom of discussion is permitted.

"Constitutional liberty" is a grand phrase, but its meaning is clear to every schoolboy and girl who plays games, because it means nothing more than freedom to play the game according to certain rules.

What is the purpose of "rules of order" for a deliberative assembly? There are three purposes. The first one is to provide an orderly way of doing things, just as in baseball the rules make it clear who is to bat, who is to pitch the ball, and who is to catch it. Thus the "rules of order" for a deliberative assembly tell you who can make a motion, who can discuss it and when it is to be voted upon.

The second purpose is to protect the rights of the minority. Since the majority can out-vote the minority, the "rules" must guarantee the right of the minority to speak against the motion and to suggest amendments to it. The minority says, "If you will first listen to our arguments against this motion, we will then be willing to accept the decision of the majority."

The third purpose is to insure reasonably prompt action by the assembly. While the minority should be permitted to talk, they should not be permitted to talk forever. The majority has rights just as much as the minority, and one important majority right is the right to come to some definite decision after the minority has had "its say."

Thus constitutional liberty for which our forefathers bled and died is now the precious heritage of every American citizen and we should all learn to use this liberty by practicing self-government according to these wonderful "rules" which our forefathers worked out for us.

Learn To Do By Doing

Citizenship training should be training in how to do things, a training of the heart (the emotions) as well as of the mind. The aggressive child should be taught to listen to the wishes of others. The timid child should be taught to express his own wishes. And all the children should be taught to deliberate as a group before they act. The tyrant is controlled only by an organized and determined majority. A tyrannical majority can be checked only by their respect for the rules of the game which we call constitutional law.

And this abiding respect for the rules of the game can be taught only by long practice in playing the game according to these rules. This is true of the rules of baseball, of hide-and-seek, of any game. It is just as true of the rules of government.

Therefore, in a representative democracy like the United States it is of the greatest importance that children be taught to govern themselves by means of a deliberative assembly just as soon as possible so that they will acquire the technique of simple legislative procedure and so that they will develop such an ingrained respect for the rights of the minority and for the orderly conduct of discussion that their "conscience" will not let them violate these "constitutional principles" later in life.

It is this technique of self-government by means of deliberative assemblies and this "ingrained respect for constitutional law" that make up the marvelous self governing capacity of the American and English people.

It is not accidental that the great self-governing peoples are also the people who play the most group games, because playing accord-

4

ing to set rules teaches one to live by set rules. If women do not have equal rights with men, what is the surest way to establish equality? By an act of a legislature changing the unequal laws? No! This has been tried and it does not work. Then what is the best way?

The best way to insure equality of rights between men and women is to have the boys and girls play competitive games together so that the girls learn to play according to the same rule as the boys and develop the habit of demanding that the rules be enforced against the boys the same as against the girls. Group games are the great enemy of inequality because they teach the principle of "one set of rules for all participants" and they establish the habit of demanding that the rules be enforced on all alike.

This manual is a simple book of rules for the conduct of group discussion, group action and group contests. By the use of the lessons and contests that go with the manual any group can learn to conduct its business in accordance with these rules after four or five one hour lessons. By the use of the contests included in these lessons this group leadership technique can be made as exciting as baseball, basketball or any other group game so that training in citizenship becomes delightful recreation instead of dry abstraction. And this kind of training establishes habits of conduct instead of platitudes to be memorized. This is scientific training for citizenship.

This is teaching representative government instead of teaching **about** it.

CONSTITUTIONAL GOVERNMENT

When we propose a law as guide,
Let all minorities deride,
For when majorities decide,
Minorities must all abide
            by this decision.

50 HORSE POWER and 50 MAN POWER

American civilization in 1830 was symbolized by the frontiersman on foot or on horseback: one man power or one horse power.

American civilization in 1930 was symbolized by the automobile, the locomotive, the aeroplane; twenty horse power, fifty horse power, five hundred horse power.

Today one man power is not enough to propel society in any direction. Twenty man power, fifty man power, five hundred man power are necessary for social achievement. That is to say, the individual must work through groups to be effective in this complex and congested society of ours. Rugged individualism has ceased to be socially useful and, therefore, is vanishing. Efficient **group leadership** must arise to take its place.

Group leadership is a social technique. This manual is designed to facilitate learning the technique for **leadership within a group.**

7

Lesson I

MAIN MOTION (or QUESTION)

The first step in learning group leadership is to arrive at an appreciation of the necessity for rules in the conduct of a group meeting. This is best and most quickly taught by having each student in turn serve as chairman. When each student serves as chairman he begins at once to learn the rules of the game because the chairman cannot say a single word without exposing his ignorance or knowledge of these rules.

Choose a teacher and have the teacher make all the motions, while some member seconds each motion made without delay. Also have the teacher announce "No discussion" (to save time) and do all the voting while each student in turn as momentary chairman states the motion just made and seconded, and asks for discussion, or puts it to vote or announces the vote and the result of the vote and then tells what is next in order for the assembly.

Each of the first four lessons should include a complete dialogue between the teacher (as the assembly) and the student chairmen so as to illustrate concretely just how each motion is used by a member of the assembly and just how it should be handled by a chairman. The following dialogue illustrates the moving and the adoption of a simple main motion (or question).

Chairman *(Student No. 1)*:—Sounds gavel or raps desk with his knuckles. "THE MEETING WILL COME TO ORDER. IS THERE ANY BUSINESS?"

Teacher *(as Assembly)*:—"MR. CHAIRMAN."

Chairman *(Student No. 2)*:—"MR. TEACHER."

Teacher *(as Assembly)*:—"I MOVE THAT WE HAVE A PARTY." Some member of the group calls out "I SECOND THE MOTION."

Chairman *(Student No. 3)*:—"IT IS MOVED AND SECONDED THAT WE HAVE A PARTY. IS THERE ANY DISCUSSION?"

Teacher *(Informally)*:—"NO DISCUSSION."

Chairman *(Student No. 4)*:—"THE VOTE IS ON THE MOTION THAT WE HAVE A PARTY. THOSE IN FAVOR SAY 'I'." *(Pause for the vote. Teacher, as Assembly, votes "I".)* "THOSE OPPOSED SAY 'NO'."

Chairman *(Student No. 5)*:—"THE 'I's' HAVE IT AND THE MOTION TO HAVE A PARTY IS CARRIED. IS THERE ANY OTHER BUSINESS?"

The main question (or motion) may be defined as any motion that may be moved when there is nothing else before the

9

assembly. By turning to page 18 in the manual any student can find, in a second, any rule on any phase of a main motion by referring to the chart at the bottom of that page.

For instance can a main motion apply to any other motion? No! (See block No. 1 at the extreme left end of the chart.) Obviously, if a main motion can be made only when there is no other motion before the assembly then there is no other motion to which the main motion can apply. Usually the main motion is of such a nature that it is an end in itself rather than a means to an end. Thus a motion "to have a picnic" is an end in itself; whereas a motion to refer to a committee is a means to an end. There must be a main motion under consideration before the motion "to refer" has any sense to it at all.

If a member desires to move a main motion ("to have a picnic," for instance) can that member interrupt another member who has the floor and is speaking to the assembly? No! (See block No. 2 on the left.) When this member desires to move "that we have a picnic," must he be recognized by the Chair before he can make his motion? Yes! (See block No. 3 on the left.)

After this member has been recognized by the Chair and has moved "that we have a picnic," must this motion be seconded before it is really before the assembly for consideration? Yes. (See block No. 4 on the left.)

When this member has been recognized by the Chair, has moved "that we have a picnic," and that motion has been seconded, must the Chair ask for discussion on this motion? Yes. (See block No. 5, the first one on the right hand page.)

When this main motion is put to a vote, how many votes are required to adopt it? A majority; that is, one more than the number of votes against it. (See block No. 6, the second one on the right hand page.)

When this motion to have a picnic has been moved, seconded and then voted down, can it be renewed, that is, can it be moved again? Not at the same meeting. But at the next meeting it can be moved again. (see block No. 7.)

When the main motion "to have a picnic" is before the assembly, what motions may apply to it? (See block No. 8.) The answer is "All," that is, any motion that can apply to other motions, such as to amend, to refer, to postpone, to close debate, to table, etc. The motion to adjourn (See page 2) does not apply to motions, it applies to the assembly. You adjourn the assembly, you do not adjourn a motion. If a main motion is before the assembly when the assembly adjourns, that main motion becomes "unfinished business" to be taken up automatically at the next session.

At the top of page 18 on the right are the rules that apply to a main motion. They cover the same points found in the chart at the bottom of the page, but these points can be found twice as quickly in the chart as they can in these more fully stated rules.

At the top of page 18-L (the page opposite 18) following the word "Member" is the correct form for moving a main motion. When rising to make a motion in a large assembly a member is always quite anxious to state it in the correct form. We are all afraid of making little mistakes that might be laughed at.

Just below this correct statement of the form of the motion is the word "Chairman" in bold-faced type. Following the word "Chairman" and in bold-faced type between quotation marks are the correct phrases which a chairman should use in stating a motion, in putting it to a vote, and in stating the vote, the result of the vote, and what is next in order for the assembly, be it an "I" vote or a "No" vote.

Thus by the use of this manual a chairman can always be sure as to what to say in each instance and as to the correct form in which he should say it. The more experienced parliamentarians are the ones who are quickest to see the advantage of this manual because they realize that the manual *never forgets and is never wrong.*" No memory is ever this reliable.

In this manual the adverb meaning yes is spelled "I" as Shakespeare spelled it instead of "Aye" as is common usage today because the word "Aye" has two pronounciations and two meanings. "Aye" pronounced "I" means "yes", but "Aye" pronounced "A" means "forever." The result is that half the people say "A" meaning "yes" and the other half say "I" meaning "yes." This leads to some confusion and frequently embarrasses the chairman who is in doubt as to which way to pronounce it. This confusion is easily avoided by spelling the adverb meaning "yes" with a capital "I" as Shakespeare did in his original editions.

For the remainder of this first recitation period the students should lay aside this lesson set and use only page 18 in the manual. As the teacher makes additional main motions and votes on them, each student in turn should read the proper phrases from page 18, inserting at the right place the motion made by the teacher. While this exercise is very simple, it should be continued until each student has served as chairman and correctly handled one step in the adoption or rejection of a main motion. If a certain student does not seem to be quite clear as to this procedure he should be required to handle each step in the procedure from the statement of the motion to its final adoption or rejection to insure that he does understand all three steps in this process.

This oral practice is fundamental in training for group leadership. Understanding the rules of procedure is not enough. A group leader must not only understand the rules, he must also be able to use them, and use them effectively. Doing depends more on the emotions than on the intellect. If, when you get up to speak, there is such a lump in your throat that you cannot speak, it makes little difference whether you know your parliamentary rules or do not know them.

Therefore, oral practice in making and, as chairman, handling these motions is absolutely essential if the student is to train his emotions so that they will function properly when he rises before the assembly to address the Chair, to make a motion, or to preside as chairman.

An effective group-leader must create in others a willingness to follow his leadership, must discipline his own emotions by much practice in order that he may inspire others to follow his leadership. In this connection it is well to remember the story of Demosthenes who was a complete failure when he first attempted to address the Athenian Assembly. But he was determined to be a leader, so he drilled and disciplined his emotions and trained his intellect until he became the greatest group leader of his day and, perhaps, the greatest orator of all time.

At the end of each lesson there should be opportunity for questions, because most people have erroneous ideas about parliamentary procedure. The student must have his erroneous ideas corrected before he can clearly understand correct procedure. However, students should not be permitted to discuss motions that have not yet been studied. It is quite foolish to attempt to teach "inside" baseball to people who do not know the simpler rules of baseball. Similarly it is a waste of time to discuss the finer points of parliamentary procedure before the simpler rules have been mastered.

It will be noted that the teacher says (informally) "No discussion" every time the chairman asks for discussion and the teacher does not desire to make another motion. This is done to save time. Ordinarily the chairman calls for discussion and then waits a minute or two for some one to discuss the motion before it is put to a vote. The teacher as the assembly just tells the chairman quickly "No discussion" so that the chairman can go ahead immediately and put the motion to a vote.

Seconding a motion is just a simple device for making sure that more than one person is sponsoring the given motion. There is no good reason why an assembly should waste time on a motion that does not have at least two sponsors.

Note:——During the first four lessons the pupils should remain in their seats. For each pupil to go to the front of the room to be chairman for just a moment is a great waste of time. The later lessons give every pupil ample opportunity to stand before the group and preside for some time.

12

Lesson II

AMENDMENTS

When the original or main motion does not exactly suit the assembly it may be changed by means of amendments before it is finally adopted or defeated. Amendments either add to, strike out, insert, or substitute (strike out and insert). Amendments may strike out or insert punctuation marks, or words, or phrases, or sentences, or paragraphs, or pages, or entire sections of a motion or bill. The procedure is the same whether you insert a comma or an entirely new section containing a thousand words.

Amendments are difficult, but they must be studied at once because they afford the only means of changing the main motion to suit the assembly. Quite frequently an important motion is adopted in a form that is undesirable simply because the members of the organization do not know how to change it to suit them. Of course educated people should know how to change motions so that they will say what the group wants them to say; consequently, a course in Group Leadership should provide a great deal of drill on amending motions.

MAIN MOTIONS AND AMENDMENTS

Chairman 1:—(Sounds gavel) "THE MEETING WILL COME TO ORDER. IS THERE ANY BUSINESS?"

Teacher:—"MR. CHAIRMAN."

Chairman 2:—"MR. TEACHER."

Teacher:"I MOVE THAT WE HAVE A PICNIC."

Some member of the group calls out, "I SECOND THE MOTION."

Chairman 3:—"IT IS MOVED AND SECONDED THAT WE HAVE A PICNIC. IS THERE ANY DISCUSSION?"

Teacher:—"MR. CHAIRMAN."

Chairman 4:—"MR. TEACHER."

Teacher:—"I MOVE THAT WE AMEND THE MOTION BY ADDING THE WORDS 'FRIDAY AFTERNOON'."

Some member calls out, "I SECOND THE AMENDMENT."

Chairman 5:—"IT IS MOVED AND SECONDED THAT WE AMEND THE MOTION BY ADDING THE WORDS 'FRIDAY AFTERNOON' SO THAT THE MOTION IF AMENDED WILL READ 'THAT WE HAVE A PICNIC FRIDAY AFTERNOON.' IS THERE ANY DISCUSSION ON THE AMENDMENT?"

Teacher:—*(informally)* "NO DISCUSSION."

Chairman 6:—"THE VOTE IS ON THE AMENDMENT THAT WE ADD THE WORDS 'FRIDAY AFTERNOON.' THOSE IN FAVOR OF THE AMENDMENT SAY 'I'." *(Pause for the vote.* Teacher votes "I".) "THOSE OPPOSED SAY 'NO'."

Chairman 7:—"THE 'I's' HAVE IT AND THE AMENDMENT IS CARRIED. THE NEXT BUSINESS IS THE MOTION AS AMENDED WHICH READS 'THAT WE HAVE A PICNIC FRIDAY AFTERNOON'. IS THERE ANY DISCUSSION ON THE *MOTION AS AMENDED?*"

Teacher:—"MR. CHAIRMAN."

Chairman 8:—"MR. TEACHER."

Teacher:—"I MOVE THAT WE AMEND THE MOTION BY ADDING THE WORDS 'AT OTTAWA PARK',"

Some member calls out, "I SECOND THE MOTION."

Chairman 9:—"IT IS MOVED AND SECONDED THAT WE AMEND THE MOTION BY ADDING THE WORDS 'AT OTTAWA PARK' SO THAT THE MOTION, IF AMENDED, WILL READ THAT WE HAVE A PICNIC FRIDAY AFTERNOON AT OTTAWA PARK. IS THERE ANY DISCUSSION ON THE AMENDMENT?"

Teacher:—*(informally)* "NO DISCUSSION."

Chairman 10:—"THE VOTE IS ON THE AMENDMENT THAT WE ADD THE WORDS 'AT OTTAWA PARK.' THOSE IN FAVOR OF THE AMENDMENT SAY 'I'." *(Pause. Teacher votes "I".)* "THOSE OPPOSED SAY 'NO'."

Chairman 11:—"THE 'I's' HAVE IT AND THE AMENDMENT IS CARRIED. THE NEXT BUSINESS IS THE *MOTION AS AMENDED* WHICH READS 'THAT WE HAVE A PICNIC FRIDAY AFTERNOON AT OTTAWA PARK.' IS THERE ANY DISCUSSION ON THE *MOTION AS AMENDED?*"

Teacher:—*(informally)* "NO DISCUSSION."

Chairman 12:—"THE VOTE IS ON THE *MOTION AS AMENDED* WHICH READS 'THAT WE HAVE A PICNIC FRIDAY AFTERNOON AT OTTAWA PARK.' THOSE IN FAVOR OF THE *MOTION AS AMENDED* SAY 'I'." *(Pause. Teacher votes "I".)* "THOSE OPPOSED SAY 'NO'."

Chairman 13:—"THE 'I's' HAVE IT AND THE *MOTION AS AMENDED* IS CARRIED. IS THERE ANY OTHER BUSINESS?"

Teacher:—"MR. CHAIRMAN."

Chairman 14:—"MR. TEACHER."

Teacher:—"I MOVE THAT WE ADJOURN."

Some member calls out:—"I SECOND THE MOTION."

Chairman 15:—"IT IS MOVED AND SECONDED THAT WE ADJOURN. THOSE IN FAVOR SAY 'I'." *(Pause. Teacher votes "I.")* "THOSE OPPOSED SAY 'NO'."

Chairman 16:—"THE 'I's' HAVE IT AND THE MOTION TO ADJOURN IS CARRIED. YOU STAND ADJOURNED. *(Chairman sounds gavel.)*

The name of the original motion is "main motion" (or question). When this original motion has been amended its name changes to "motion as amended" just as Miss Mary Brown's name changes to Mrs. J. H. Smith when she marries Mr. J. H. Smith. And if Mr. Smith dies and Mrs. Smith marries Mr. Fred Johnson we still call her by the name of her present husband, that is, Mrs. Fred Johnson. We do not call her Mrs. Smith-Johnson. To do so would be awkward and unnecessary. In the same way we call the amended motion simply the "motion as amended" regardless of whether it has been amended once or a dozen times.

For similar reasons of convenience the form for amending a motion that has already been amended is *not* "I move that we amend the motion as amended." On the contrary, the form of the motion to amend is the same regardless of whether it applies to an original motion or to a motion as amended. Thus the unvarying form for the motion to amend is "I move that we amend the motion (resolution or bill) by —." Persons ignorant of proper parliamentary procedure frequently "move to amend" the motion so that it will read as follows:—Then they read the main motion the way they want it to read. This requires the chairman and secretary to formulate the amendment in proper form. This is a bad practice, first, because it does not always make it clear just what changes are being made in the original motion; second, because it delegates to the secretary and chairman the task of officially wording the amendment that is to go into the minutes. They might abuse this power by wording the amendment to suit themselves and not as the mover of the amendment meant it to be.

When the chairman is in doubt as to the wording of an amendment he may require the mover of the amendment to present it in writing. Also, the chairman may declare an amendment out of order if it is a ridiculous amendment, or if its meaning is not clear. The chairman should never ask the assembly to vote on a motion or amendment which he does not understand or which they do not understand.

Many people believe that when a main motion is before the assembly and someone moves an amendment to it, the main motion must be voted on first. This is, of course, just one hundred per cent wrong. *The main motion is always the last motion to be voted on.* The biblical phrase that "the first shall be last and the last shall be first" applies to motions in an assembly. A main motion cannot be moved except when there are no other motions before the assembly. Therefore, at that moment it is the first and only motion before the house. If, now, certain subsidiary, incidental or privileged motions are moved (as they may be; see Classes of Motions page XIII in manual) they are the last motions to come before the assembly but they are the motions that must be voted on first. For instance, the motion to adjourn is nearly always in order and when moved must be voted on at once without debate (except when no time has been fixed for the next meeting). See motion to adjourn, (page 2, rule 7).

Note:—The following motions and amendments are suggested for use by the teacher in continuing the drill on main motions and amendments while the student-chairmen handle them properly by using page 18 and page 16 in the manual.

I move that we have a picnic.

I move that we amend the motion by adding the words,
"in Ottawa Park."
"Friday afternoon."
"at 4 o'clock."

I move that we have a Halloween party.

I move that we amend the motion by adding the words,
"October 30th."
"in the gymnasium."

Or, I move that we amend the motion by striking out the word "party" and inserting the word "picnic."

Or, I move that we insert the word "pot-luck" before the word "picnic."

The shorter and simpler the motions and amendments, the quicker each student will learn the principle involved in amending motions. Long motions and long amendments consume much time but they involve exactly the same rules as short motions and short amendments. In these first lessons the attention should be concentrated on the rules of procedure involved and not on the content of the motions or amendments proposed.

Most main motions contain two or more ideas. For instance the motion "to have annual dues of one dollar" contains both the idea of "having annual dues" and the further idea "that these dues be one dollar." Now some of the members of the club may be very much in favor of annual dues but they are opposed to dues of one dollar. If they vote "No" on this motion it indicates that they are opposed to annual dues. But if they move to amend the motion by striking out the words, "one dollar" and inserting the words "fifty cents," it indicates that they favor annual dues but that they think the amount should be only "fifty cents." By voting on the amendment first they come to agreement as to "how much the dues ought to be." Then they vote on the "motion as amended," and if the "motion as amended" is carried by majority vote the club has decided "that there shall be annual dues" and "that these dues shall be fifty cents." Any member opposed to all annual dues should have voted against the amendment and against the main motion.

A motion to have a picnic involves two ideas, the first idea is that we have some kind of a good time, and the second idea is that this good time be in the form of a picnic. Those that desire some kind of a good time but prefer a dance to a picnic should move to amend the motion by striking out the word "picnic" and inserting the word "dance." Still other members may not care whether it is a picnic or a dance provided it is on Saturday when they can go. They are in favor of any kind of a good time if it is to be on Saturday, but they are opposed if it is to be on Friday. Therefore, these members want it determined definitely as to *what* it is to be and *when* it is to be before they vote on the original motion (as amended) "that we have a good time in the form of a picnic Saturday afternoon."

It is true that the club could vote first on a main motion "that we have some kind of a good time." Then, if that was carried by majority vote, someone could move that we have a picnic. (This would be a main motion because there is nothing else before the assembly since the motion to have a good time has already been carried and is, therefore, no longer before the assembly.) If the motion to have a picnic is carried, then someone could move another main motion "that the time for this picnic be Saturday afternoon."

But isn't it better to settle these questions of the *kind* of a good time, the *day* and the *place* by amendments to the original motion so that when the original motion as amended is voted on finally the club will have determined all of these points by one main motion (with, of course, the necessary amendments)!

I.

I am debatable and I require a second.
I require a majority vote only.
I can be amended.
What am I?

2.

I am debatable and I require a second.
My mover must first be recognized by the Chair.
I am used to change other motions.
What am I?

3.

I am debatable and require a second.
I cannot be applied to other motions.
I am an end in myself.
What am I?

Lesson III

SUBSIDIARY MOTIONS

If a member moves that your organization buy a piano, it may be quite unwise to decide that question at once. Perhaps no one present knows just how much a piano costs. Perhaps no one knows whether there is money enough in the treasury to make such a purchase, or whether you would be permitted to use a piano if you had one. In such a case the thing to do is to refer this question to a committee for investigation and report before final action is taken.

Similarly, some one may move that you buy a radio. Although the mover of the motion may know what a radio will cost and can tell how much each member will have to be assessed to pay for it, the group as a whole may still desire a few days to think this over before a final vote is taken. In such a case the thing to do is to move that the consideration of the proposition of buying a radio be postponed until the next meeting.

On the other hand when some one moves that your organization take out a Red Cross membership at the cost of one dollar, practically every one may be in favor of the motion and willing to vote on it at once, nevertheless, two members may get into such a heated discussion on the subject that it may look as though their discussion will last all day. In this case the large majority in favor of taking out this Red Cross membership may become impatient at the long discussion and "move to close debate." If this motion is carried by a two-thirds vote, debate is stopped at once and the group can then vote on the main motion "to take out a membership in the Red Cross at a cost of one dollar."

These motions that serve to temporarily dispose of a main motion or limit debate on it are called *subsidiary motions* because they have no purpose other than to affect the main motion. In other words, these motions are subsidiary to the main motion. Strictly speaking, an amendment is a subsidiary motion because an amendment has no purpose other than to change another motion.

The subsidiary motions are "to lay on the table," "to close debate," "to postpone to a certain day," "to refer," "to amend."

Subsidiary motions (except to amend) are quite simple both in their wording and in their effect; consequently, one practice should be sufficient for achieving a preliminary mastery over them.

Chairman 1:—"THE MEETING WILL COME TO ORDER. IS THERE ANY BUSINESS?"

Teacher:—*(as the assembly)*:—"MR. CHAIRMAN."

Chairman 2:—"MR. TEACHER."

Teacher:—"I MOVE THAT WE HAVE A SCHOOL BAND."

Someone calls out, "I SECOND THE MOTION."

Chairman 3:—"IT IS MOVED AND SECONDED THAT WE HAVE A SCHOOL BAND. IS THERE ANY DISCUSSION?"

Teacher:—"MR. CHAIRMAN."

Chairman 4:—"MR. TEACHER."

Teacher:—"I MOVE THAT WE REFER THIS MATTER TO THE MUSIC COMMITTEE."

Someone calls out, "I SECOND THE MOTION."

Chairman 5:—"IT IS MOVED AND SECONDED THAT WE REFER THIS MATTER TO THE MUSIC COMMITTEE. IS THERE ANY DISCUSSION?"

Teacher:—*(informally)* "NO DISCUSSION."

Chairman 6:—"THE VOTE IS ON THE MOTION TO REFER THIS MATTER OF A SCHOOL BAND TO THE MUSIC COMMITTEE. THOSE IN FAVOR OF THE MOTION TO REFER SAY 'I'." *(Pause. Teacher votes "I.")* "THOSE OPPOSED SAY 'NO'."

Chairman 7:—"THE 'I's' HAVE IT AND THE MOTION TO REFER IS CARRIED. THE SECRETARY WILL REFER THIS MATTER OF A SCHOOL BAND TO THE MUSIC COMMITTEE FOR INVESTIGATION AND REPORT. IS THERE ANY FURTHER BUSINESS?"

Teacher:—"MR. CHAIRMAN."

Chairman 8:—"MR. TEACHER."

Teacher:—"I MOVE THAT WE HAVE A CLASS PIN."

Someone calls out, "I SECOND THE MOTION."

Chairman 9:—"IT IS MOVED AND SECONDED THAT WE HAVE A CLASS PIN. IS THERE ANY DISCUSSION?"

Teacher:—"MR. CHAIRMAN."

Chairman 10:—"MR. TEACHER."

Teacher:—" I DO NOT KNOW JUST WHAT SUCH A PIN WOULD COST. PERHAPS WE SHOULD POSTPONE CONSIDERATION OF THIS MATTER UNTIL WE CAN LEARN THE PROBABLE COST. THEREFORE,

I MOVE THAT WE POSTPONE CONSIDERATION OF THIS MOTION UNTIL THE NEXT MEETING."

Someone calls out, "I SECOND THE MOTION."

Chairman 11:—"IT IS MOVED AND SECONDED THAT WE POSTPONE CONSIDERATION OF THIS MOTION ABOUT A CLASS PIN UNTIL THE NEXT MEETING. IS THERE ANY DISCUSSION AS TO THE ADVISABILITY OF POSTPONEMENT?"

Teacher:—*(informally)* "NO DISCUSSION."

Chairman 12:—"THE VOTE IS ON THE MOTION TO POSTPONE CONSIDERATION OF THIS CLASS PIN PROPOSITION UNTIL THE NEXT MEETING. THOSE IN FAVOR OF POSTPONEMENT TILL THE NEXT MEETING SAY 'I'." *(Pause. Teacher votes "I".)* "THOSE OPPOSED SAY 'NO'."

Chairman 13:—"THE 'I's' HAVE IT AND THE MOTION TO POSTPONE CONSIDERATION UNTIL THE NEXT MEETING IS CARRIED. IS THERE ANY OTHER BUSINESS?"

Teacher:—"MR. CHAIRMAN."

Chairman 14:—"MR. TEACHER."

Teacher:—"I MOVE THAT WE HAVE A LITERARY SOCIETY."

Someone calls out, "I SECOND THE MOTION."

Chairman 15:—"IT IS MOVED AND SECONDED THAT WE HAVE A LITERARY SOCIETY. IS THERE ANY DISCUSSION?"

Teacher:—"MR. CHAIRMAN."

Chairman 16:—"MR. TEACHER."

Teacher:—"IT IS ABOUT TIME FOR THIS MEETING TO CLOSE. NEVERTHELESS, THIS QUESTION OF A LITERARY SOCIETY SHOULD BE THOROUGHLY DISCUSSED BEFORE WE TAKE FINAL ACTION ON IT. THERE IS ANOTHER MATTER THAT SHOULD BE DECIDED IMMEDIATELY. THEREFORE, I MOVE THAT WE LAY THIS MOTION TO HAVE A LITERARY SOCIETY ON THE TABLE. WE CAN TAKE IT FROM THE TABLE LATER WHEN WE HAVE MORE TIME FOR IT."

Someone calls out, "I SECOND THE MOTION TO LAY ON THE TABLE."

Chairman 17:—"IT IS MOVED AND SECONDED THAT WE TABLE THE MOTION TO HAVE A LITERARY SOCIETY. THOSE IN FAVOR OF THE MOTION TO TABLE SAY 'I'." *(Pause. Teacher votes "I.")* "THOSE OPPOSED 'NO'."

Chairman 18:—"THE 'I's' HAVE IT AND THE MOTION TO TABLE IS CARRIED. THE MOTION TO HAVE A LITERARY SOCIETY IS TABLED. IS THERE ANY FURTHER BUSINESS?"

Teacher:—"MR. CHAIRMAN."

Chairman 19:—"MR. TEACHER."

Teacher:—"THE URGENT MATTER I REFERRED TO A WHILE AGO IS AN INVITATION TO ATTEND THE SHAKESPERIAN PLAY TONIGHT AT THE AUDITORIUM. FREE TICKETS FOR THE ENTIRE CLASS ARE AVAILABLE IF YOU DECIDE TO GO. I MOVE THAT WE ACCEPT THE INVITATION TO ATTEND THE SHAKESPERIAN PLAY AT THE AUDITORIUM TONIGHT."

Someone calls out, "I SECOND THE MOTION."

Chairman 20:—"IT IS MOVED AND SECONDED THAT WE ACCEPT THE INVITATION TO ATTEND THE SHAKESPERIAN PLAY TONIGHT AT THE AUDITORIUM. IS THERE ANY DISCUSSION?"

Teacher:—"MR. CHAIRMAN."

Chairman 21:—"MR. TEACHER."

Teacher:—"SINCE THE TIME IS SO SHORT FOR DECIDING THIS MATTER, I MOVE THAT WE CLOSE DEBATE AND VOTE IMMEDIATELY ON THE PENDING QUESTION."

Someone calls out, "I SECOND THE MOTION."

Chairman 22:—"IT IS MOVED AND SECONDED THAT WE CLOSE DEBATE AND VOTE IMMEDIATELY ON THE PENDING QUESTION. THOSE IN FAVOR OF THE MOTION TO CLOSE DEBATE SAY 'I'." *(Pause. Teacher votes 12 "I's.")* "THOSE OPPOSED SAY 'NO'." *(Pause. Teacher votes 6 "Noes.")*

Chairman 23:—"THE VOTE IS 'I's' 12, 'Noes' 6. THE 'I's' HAVE IT BY A TWO-THIRDS VOTE AND THE MOTION TO CLOSE DEBATE IS CARRIED. THE NEXT BUSINESS IS THE VOTE ON THE MOTION THAT WE ACCEPT THE INVITATION TO ATTEND THE

SHAKESPERIAN PLAY TONIGHT AT THE AUDI-
TORIUM. THOSE IN FAVOR OF THIS MOTION SAY
'I'." *(Pause. Teacher votes "I.")* "THOSE OPPOSED SAY
'NO'."

Chairman 24:—"THE 'I's' HAVE IT AND THE MOTION TO
ACCEPT THE INVITATION TO THE SHAKESPER-
IAN PLAY TONIGHT IS CARRIED. IS THERE ANY
FURTHER BUSINESS?"

Teacher:—"MR. CHAIRMAN."

Chairman 25:—"MR. TEACHER."

Teacher:—"I MOVE THAT WE TAKE FROM THE TABLE
THE MOTION TO HAVE A LITERARY SOCIETY."

Someone calls out, "I SECOND THE MOTION."

Cairman 26:—"IT IS MOVED AND SECONDED THAT WE
TAKE FROM THE TABLE THE MOTION TO HAVE
A LITERARY SOCIETY. THOSE IN FAVOR OF THE
MOTION TO TAKE FROM THE TABLE SAY 'I'."
(Pause. Teacher votes "I.") "THOSE OPPOSED SAY 'NO'."

Chairman 27:—"THE 'I's' HAVE IT AND THE MOTION TO
TAKE FROM THE TABLE IS CARRIED. YOU NOW
HAVE BEFORE YOU THE MOTION THAT WE HAVE
A LITERARY SOCIETY. IS THERE ANY DISCUS-
SION ON THE MOTION THAT WE HAVE A LIT-
ERARY SOCIETY?"

Teacher:—"MR. CHAIRMAN."

Chairman 28:—"MR. TEACHER."

Teacher:—"I SEE BY MY WATCH THAT IT IS TIME FOR
THE BELL, THEREFORE, I MOVE THAT WE AD-
JOURN."

Someone calls out, "I SECOND THE MOTION."

Chairman 29:—"IT IS MOVED AND SECONDED THAT WE
ADJOURN. THOSE IN FAVOR OF ADJOURNMENT
SAY 'I'." *(Pause. Teacher votes "I.")* "THOSE OPPOSED
SAY 'NO'."

Chairman 30:—"THE 'I's' HAVE IT AND THE MOTION TO
ADJOURN IS CARRIED. YOU STAND ADJOURNED."
(Chairman sounds gavel.)

Note:—Since the motion to adjourn was passed when the motion
to have a literary society was pending, this motion is "unfinished
business" to be taken up at the next meeting.

Obviously the motion to close debate deprives the minority of their opportunity to discuss the motion. However, this arbitrary "steam-rolling" of the minority is permitted only when supported by a two-thirds majority. One of the main purposes of parliamentary law is to protect the rights of the minority. On the other hand, the assembly must have the power at times to speed up business by closing debate. But if the two-thirds majority uses its power to close debate too often and thus deprives the minority of all opportunity to present the other side of questions, the minority will soon refuse to participate in the work of the assembly. Fair play is good politics.

This exercise should be continued by the teacher making new motions and then moving one of the subsidiary motions and voting "I" on each one. The student chairman need only turn to pages 12, 13, 14, 15, 16, or 17 in the manual to find on the left hand page the chairman's phrases for handling any subsidiary motion.

Much drill on the use of these subsidiary motions is advisable because they are used a great deal by any intelligent assembly. However, care should be taken not to move a second subsidiary motion until the first one has been voted on because this would raise the question of precedence of subsidiary motions, and this question is reserved for the next lesson.

The next assignment should include a written memory test on the name of the motions on pages 12 to 18 in the manual. The next lesson on precedence of motions loses much of its value unless the students have memorized this sequence.

Note:—The motion to postpone indefinitely has quite a different purpose from the other subsidiary motions and, therefore, is explained and its use illustrated in lesson X on Parliamentary Strategy.

The motion "objection to consideration" is sometimes classed as a subsidiary motion. This difficult motion is not often used, but it is of great value in certain abnormal situations. (See lesson XIII.) It is classified here as an "incidental motion," but its exact classification is not important so long as its definite purpose and highly specialized precedence are clear.

Lesson IV

PRECEDENCE OF MOTIONS

The wise rule is that a group of people should never attempt to talk about more than one thing at a time. This is why we can have only one main motion (main question) before the class at one time. Obviously it would be unwise to move that we organize a literary society, and then, before deciding this question, let someone move that we have a picnic Saturday afternoon.

But this rule that only one main motion can be considered at one time does not apply to subsidiary motions. The reason why more than one subsidiary motion can be before the class at one time is that subsidiary motions provide ways of changing or disposing of the main motion, and the first method suggested for disposing of the main motion may not be as quick or as satisfactory as another method.

For example, if we move to have a picnic Saturday afternoon someone may want to know where we are going to have it. To answer this question a member may move to amend the motion by adding the words "in Ottawa Park." While the class is discussing the advantages of having the picnic at Ottawa Park rather than at Walbridge Park, some member may think that this whole proposal should be referred to a "picnic committee" so that they can make all arrangements for transportation, food, games, etc. Then while this motion "to refer to a committee" is being discussed someone notices that it is almost time for the class bell to ring and close the meeting. In order to get this matter settled before the bell rings this member may move "to close debate." If this motion "to close debate" is carried by a two-thirds vote, the chairman can then call for a vote on the motion "to refer to a committee" at once without giving anyone else a chance to discuss it.

If this motion "to refer to a committee" is carried, then the whole picnic proposition is turned over to the "picnic committee." If the motion "to refer to the committee" is lost, the chairman will call for a vote on the amendment to add the words "in Ottawa Park." Then if this amendment is carried, the chairman will call for a vote on the motion as amended which is that we "have a picnic Saturday afternoon in Ottawa Park."

Obviously, there would be confusion if one could move any of these subsidiary motions at any time. Public schools have learned the importance of having fire drills so that in case of fire all the students will not attempt to go through the door at the same time. Instead of all rushing to the door at once, the students line up in marching order and then those ahead go through first while those at the rear go through last.

It is the same way with subsidiary motions. Some rank above

others. Those of low rank yield their place, if need be, to those of high rank just as a young gentleman steps back and permits a lady or an elderly gentleman to precede him into the room, or gets up and yields his seat to them if they need a seat.

This order of rank or *precedence* for subsidiary motions has been worked out by a thousand years of legislative experience in England and America. This order of precedence has been found to work better than any other. It is as follows in the order named:

To lay on the table, or "to table,"

To limit or close debate,

To postpone to a certain day, or "to postpone definitely,"

To refer,

To amend.

Thus if it is moved to have a picnic and then it is moved to refer this to a committee, a motion to amend the main motion is not in order until the motion to refer has been voted down, because the motion to refer has precedence over the motion to amend the main motion. Or, stated the other way, the motion to refer does not yield to the motion to amend the main motion.

When someone makes a motion that is not in order the chairman says, "Your motion is out of order." Then the chairman proceeds just as though this improper motion had never been moved.

If someone moves that we have an entertainment, then someone moves to amend it by adding the words "a week from Friday," and in the discussion the members ask what kind of an entertainment, how long shall it last, who is to take part in it, etc., it may become evident that the entire class is too large a group to decide efficiently all of these details. Consequently someone may move "that this entire proposal be referred to a committee of five to be appointed by the chairman," Such a committee could learn what day would be best for this entertainment. They could learn just how much time would be allowed for it, and they could draw up an outline program for the class to consider before finally deciding whether to have an entertainment or not.

In this case the motion to refer is in order even though the motion to amend the main motion is before the assembly, because the motion to amend the main motion yields to the motion to refer. The reason for this is that when there are many details to settle in connection with a main question like having a picnic or an entertainment, a committee can work out these many details better than they can be worked out by the assembly (class) as a whole through the slow process of amending the main motion as many times as there are details to be worked out.

The motion "to lay on the table" takes precedence over all other subsidiary motions because it enables the assembly to lay aside quickly any main motion in order to do something else that the assembly thinks is more important or more interesting. Since the chief purpose of this motion is to enable the assembly to quickly lay aside the main motion, the motion to lay on the table is not debatable. Thus the motion to "table the main motion" can be made even though all the other subsidiary motions are before the assembly, and it can be put to a vote just as soon as it is moved because it is not debatable.

CHAIRMANSHIP

When a member of the assembly makes a motion that is "out of order," it is the duty of the chairman to declare it "out of order."

A chairman should keep the manual open before him so as to tell at a glance whether the motion just moved is in order or not. (See footnote below.) The secretary should assist in this matter of precedence by calling the chairman's attention to improper motions when he fails to call them "out of order."

An assembly may become quite excited if the chairman declares a motion "out of order" when, as a matter of fact, it is "in order," or accepts a motion as "in order" when it should have been declared "out of order." Organized groups become disorganized most frequently because of incompetent chairmen.

The chairman, like an umpire of a baseball game, must know the rules and must apply these rules quickly, firmly, and impartially. A good chairman inspires the assembly with pride in its own efficiency and dignity. A weak and vascillating or ignorant chairman humiliates the assembly because of the resulting lack of dignity and efficiency.

Footnote:— In the manual the motions from 1 to 18 are listed in their order of precedence so that any motion above takes precedence over any motion below it on that side, and all motions on the left side take precedence over any motion on the right side (except for certain special situations that seldom arise). (See the rules under each motion.) Stating this general rule in terms of the page number in the manual, all motions of larger page number yield to motions with a smaller page number. Conversely, a motion with a smaller page number takes precedence over a motion with a larger page number. Thus the motion on page 1 has the highest precedence of all, while the motion on page 18 has the lowest precedence. The motions on pages 19 and 20 can not be classified in this simple manner for reasons that will be obvious a little later.

The heavy black line at the top of page 19 is to show the "bottom of precedence." That is to say, the main question (or motion) has the lowest possible precedence. The two motions below this line are "unclassified motions" because their precedence cannot be fitted into the above order of precedence for reasons that will be explained in the lesson on "To Reconsider." (See lesson XI.)

This lesson is to teach chairmen how to handle motions that are "out of order" and to provide additional practice in the use of subsidiary motions.

Chairman 1:—"THE MEETING WILL COME TO ORDER. IS THERE ANY BUSINESS?"

Teacher:—"MR. CHAIRMAN."

Chairman 2:—"MR. TEACHER."

Teacher:—"I MOVE THAT WE HAVE A LITERARY SOCIETY."

Someone calls out, "I SECOND THE MOTION."

Chairman 3:—"IT IS MOVED AND SECONDED THAT WE HAVE A LITERARY SOCIETY. IS THERE ANY DISCUSSION?"

Teacher:—"MR. CHAIRMAN."

Chairman 4:—"MR. TEACHER."

Teacher:—"I MOVE THAT WE REFER THIS QUESTION OF A LITERARY SOCIETY TO THE ENTERTAINMENT COMMITTEE."

Someone calls out, "I SECOND THE MOTION."

Chairman 5:—"IT IS MOVED AND SECONDED THAT WE REFER THIS QUESTION OF A LITERARY SOCIETY TO THE ENTERTAINMENT COMMITTEE. IS THERE ANY DISCUSSION ON THE MOTION TO REFER?"

Teacher:—"MR. CHAIRMAN."

Chairman 6:—"MR. TEACHER."

Teacher:—"I MOVE THAT WE AMEND THE MOTION TO HAVE A LITERARY SOCIETY BY ADDING THE WORDS 'TO MEET ON FRIDAY AFTERNOONS'."

Someone calls out, "I SECOND THE AMENDMENT."

Chairman 7:—"THIS AMENDMENT IS OUT OF ORDER BECAUSE THERE IS A MOTION TO REFER BEFORE THE ASSEMBLY AND THE MOTION TO REFER DOES NOT YIELD TO THE MOTION TO AMEND THE MAIN MOTION. IS THERE ANY DISCUSSION ON THE MOTION TO REFER?"

Teacher:— (informally) "NO DISCUSSION."

Chairman 8:—"THE VOTE IS ON THE MOTION TO REFER TO THE ENTERTAINMENT COMMITTEE. THOSE IN FAVOR OF THE MOTION TO REFER SAY 'I'." (Pause. Teacher votes "I.") "THOSE OPPOSED SAY 'NO'."

Chairman 9:—"THE 'I's' HAVE IT AND THE MOTION TO REFER IS CARRIED. IS THERE ANY OTHER BUSINESS?"

Teacher:—"MR. CHAIRMAN."

Chairman 10:—"MR. TEACHER."

Teacher:—"I MOVE THAT WE HAVE AN ORCHESTRA."

Someone calls out, "I SECOND THE MOTION."

Chairman 11:—"IT IS MOVED AND SECONDED THAT WE HAVE AN ORCHESTRA. IS THERE ANY DISCUSSION?"

Teacher:—"MR. CHAIRMAN."

Chairman 12:—"MR. TEACHER."

Teacher:"I MOVE THAT WE POSTPONE CONSIDERATION OF THIS MOTION UNTIL NEXT FRIDAY."

Someone calls out, "I SECOND THE MOTION."

Chairman 13:—"IT IS MOVED AND SECONDED THAT WE POSTPONE UNTIL FRIDAY THE CONSIDERATION OF THE MOTION TO HAVE AN ORCHESTRA. IS THERE ANY DISCUSSION AS TO THE ADVISABILITY OF POSTPONEMENT?"

Teacher:—"MR. CHAIRMAN."

Chairman 14:—"MR. TEACHER."

Teacher:—"I MOVE THAT WE REFER THIS QUESTION OF AN ORCHESTRA TO THE MUSIC COMMITTEE."

Chairman 15:—"YOUR MOTION IS OUT OF ORDER. THE MOTION TO POSTPONE TO A CERTAIN DAY DOES NOT YIELD TO THE MOTION TO REFER. IS THERE ANY FURTHER DISCUSSION AS TO THE ADVISABILITY OF POSTPONEMENT UNTIL FRIDAY?"

Teacher:—"MR. CHAIRMAN."

Chairman 16:—"MR. TEACHER."

Teacher:—"I MOVE THAT WE CLOSE DEBATE AND VOTE IMMEDIATELY ON THE PENDING QUESTION."

Someone calls out, "I SECOND THE MOTION."

Chairman 17:—"IT IS MOVED AND SECONDED THAT WE CLOSE DEBATE AND VOTE IMMEDIATELY ON THE PENDING QUESTION. THOSE IN FAVOR OF CLOSING DEBATE SAY 'I'." *(Pause. Teacher votes "I, I, I" (3 I's).)* "THOSE OPPOSED SAY 'NO'." *(Teacher votes "No" (one No only).)*

Chairman 18:—"THE VOTE IS 'I's' 3, 'NOES' 1. THE 'I's' HAVE IT BY A TWO-THIRDS VOTE AND THE MOTION TO CLOSE DEBATE IS CARRIED. THE NEXT BUSINESS IS THE VOTE ON THE MOTION TO POSTPONE CONSIDERATION UNTIL FRIDAY. THOSE IN FAVOR OF THE MOTION TO POSTPONE UNTIL FRIDAY SAY 'I'. (Pause.) THOSE OPPOSED SAY 'NO'." (Teacher votes "No.")

Chairman 19:—"THE 'NOES' HAVE IT AND THE MOTION TO POSTPONE UNTIL FRIDAY IS LOST. IS THERE ANY FURTHER DISCUSSION ON THE MOTION TO HAVE AN ORCHESTRA?"

Teacher:—"MR. CHAIRMAN."

Chairman 20:—"MR. TEACHER."

Teacher:—"THIS MOTION TO HAVE AN ORCHESTRA HAS TAKEN UP TOO MUCH TIME ALREADY. IN ORDER THAT WE MAY TAKE UP SOME OTHER MATTERS OF MORE IMPORTANCE I MOVE THAT WE LAY ON THE TABLE THIS MOTION TO HAVE AN ORCHESTRA."

Someone calls out, "I SECOND THE MOTION."

Chairman 21:—"IT IS MOVED AND SECONDED THAT WE TABLE THE MOTION TO HAVE AN ORCHESTRA. THOSE IN FAVOR OF THE MOTION TO TABLE SAY 'I'. (Pause) THOSE OPPOSED SAY 'NO'." (Teacher votes "No.")

Chairman 22:—"THE 'NOES' HAVE IT AND THE MOTION TO TABLE IS LOST. IS THERE ANY FURTHER DISCUSSION ON THE MOTION TO HAVE AN ORCHESTRA?"

Teacher:—"MR. CHAIRMAN."

Chairman 23:—"MR. TEACHER."

Teacher:—"I MOVE THAT WE ADJOURN."

Someone calls out, "I SECOND THE MOTION."

Chairman 24:—"IT IS MOVED AND SECONDED THAT WE ADJOURN. THOSE IN FAVOR OF ADJOURNMENT SAY 'I'. (Pause) THOSE OPPOSED SAY 'NO'." (Teacher votes "No.")

Chairman 25:—"THE 'NOES' HAVE IT AND THE MOTION TO ADJOURN IS LOST. IS THERE ANY FURTHER DISCUSSION ON THE MOTION TO HAVE AN ORCHESTRA?"

Teacher:—(*informally*) "NO DISCUSSION."

Chairman 26:—"THE VOTE IS ON THE MOTION THAT WE HAVE AN ORCHESTRA. THOSE IN FAVOR OF HAVING AN ORCHESTRA SAY 'I'. (*Pause*) THOSE OPPOSED SAY 'NO'." (*Teacher votes "No."*)

Chairman 27:—"THE 'NOES' HAVE IT AND THE MOTION TO HAVE AN ORCHESTRA IS LOST. IS THERE ANY FURTHER BUSINESS?" (*After a pause*) "IF NOT, A MOTION TO ADJOURN IS IN ORDER."

Teacher:—"MR. CHAIRMAN."

Chairman 28:—"MR. TEACHER."

Teacher:—"I MOVE THAT WE ADJOURN."

Someone calls out, "I SECOND IT."

Chairman 29:—"IT IS MOVED AND SECONDED THAT WE ADJOURN. THOSE IN FAVOR SAY 'I'." (*Teacher votes "I."*) "THOSE OPPOSED SAY 'NO'."

Chairman 30:—"THE 'I's' HAVE IT AND THE MOTION TO ADJOURN IS CARRIED. YOU STAND ADJOURNED." (*Sounds gavel.*)

After giving the students ample opportunity to ask questions, the drill should be continued by having the students use their manuals while the teacher makes additional main motions and then disposes of them by the use of subsidiary motions. Occasionally the teacher should make subsidiary motions that are out of order so that the chairmen may become accustomed to watching the precedence of motions as well as the mere phraseology of handling motions that are in order.

For this more complicated drill the teacher should serve as secretary also by writing each motion as made on the blackboard. At this point it is well to begin teaching certain elements of note-taking for "the minutes" by diagraming the relation of each subsidiary or privileged motion to the motion or motions already pending. For example:—

Main motion— to have a picnic.
Amendment—
                   Friday afternoon
           Refer to entertainment comm.
(*See Lesson* XVII
on Secretaryship)
             Close Debate
       Adjourn

The rule that the same main motion may not be moved twice in the same meeting should be ignored in these early drill lessons so that the teacher (as the assembly) will not have to worry too much about thinking up new motions. In fact, this rule should not be enforced until the class begins to keep regular minutes of each meeting and has these minutes read and approved at the next meeting.

TO ADJOURN

The motion to adjourn is a "privileged motion"; that is, it can be moved while other motions are pending. The reason for this is that the assembly must have control of its own adjournment. It would be silly indeed for an assembly to continue to sit in a cold room or a smoke-filled room simply because the motion to adjourn was not in order. Therefore, the general rule is that the simple motion to adjourn is practically always in order.

But if this motion to adjourn is qualified, that is, if the motion reads "that we adjourn at ten-thirty," then this qualified motion is not privileged and can be moved only when no other motion is pending.

Another feature of the motion to adjourn is that it does not apply to any other motion. You do not adjourn a motion, you adjurn an assembly. It is the meeting that adjourns.

The effect of adjournment is to make all pending motions "unfinished business" that should be brought up at the next meeting as "unfinished business."

CHAIRMANSHIP CONTEST

The class is divided into two sides as in a spelling match, each student having a manual in his hand. The teacher makes motions, has some student second them all to save time, then announces no discussion, and votes as she pleases, while each student chairman in turn (alternating between the sides as in a spelling match) handles each motion as a good chairman should. When a chairman makes a mistake or delays too long he "goes down." This continues until all of one side are "down."

The chairman should have a good secretary to write the motions on the blackboard as they are moved. (See lesson XVII on Secretaryship.)

A good way to reverse this contest so as to give the poorer chairmen the most practice is to provide that instead of the one making a mistake as chairman or taking too much time "going down," the chairman who handles the motion promptly and correctly "goes down" while those who are too slow or make mistakes remain standing and, therefore, get the additional practice that they need. Under this rule it is, of course, the side that "goes down" first that wins.

This latter form of chairmanship contest is excellent as a means of guaranteeing that the slowest member of the class really understands the procedure for handling the different motions before going on to the next lesson in which the students themselves make the motions.

PARLIAMENTARY CHARADES

I.

I am very useful in speeding up business.
I may apply to any debatable motion.
I yield to the motion to table.
I require a two-thirds vote.
What am I?

2.

I am useful when the assembly wants to get rid of a main
    motion quickly.
I am not debatable but I require a majority vote only.
I take precedence over all other subsidiary motions.
What am I?

3.

I am useful when the main motion involves too many details.
I may be amended and I am debatable.
I cannot be applied to subsidiary motions.
I yield to the motion to postpone definitely.
What am I?

4.

I am useful when the original motion is not quite satisfactory.
I am debatable and I require a second.
I yield to all other subsidiary motions.
What am I?

5.

I am useful when the assembly is not yet ready to decide on
    the main motion.
I am debatable and I may be amended.
I take precedence over the motion to refer.
I yield to the motion to close debate.
What am I?

33

Lesson V
RELAY CONTEST

In a relay race two groups compete by running, but only one member of each group can run at one time. This same scheme may be utilized for a parliamentary contest. The teacher serves as chairman with a student as secretary to keep track of the motions made. When the teacher as chairman calls the meeting to order and asks, "Is there any business?" the first student on either team may be recognized by the Chair to make a motion. If the Chair recognizes number one on the "A" team first and he moves "that we have a dance," then the "A" team is ahead. It is then a contest between number two on the "A" team and number one on the "B" team to see which one can get recognized by the Chair in order to "amend" this motion or to refer it to a committee. If number one of the "B" team is recognized by the Chair and amends the motion, then it is a race between number two of each team to see who gets recognized first so as to move that the motion be referred to a committee or to move some other subsidiary motion. Thus each member in turn must make a proper motion that is in order before the next member of his team can make a motion. The first side to have all its members participate in a proper parliamentary manner wins the contest. Seconding a motion is such a simple act that it is not considered in this contest. Therefore, anyone can second the motions made and someone should second each motion quite promptly to avoid unnecessary delay.

It should be made clear to the students that a chairman is an umpire applying the rules as best he can. It should also be made clear that just as an umpire in a baseball game can have no "tie" decisions, (he must call it a ball or a strike, he must call the batter safe or out) just so must the chairman recognize one person as having the right to the floor even though two persons stand up and address the Chair at exactly the same moment. As a matter of common fairness the chairman should recognize first one side and then the other when members from both sides continue to rise and address the Chair at exactly the same time. When, however, members of one side obviously are rising and addressing the Chair a second or two ahead of the other side, the chairman should continue to recognize the member who rises and addresses the Chair first even though this means that the slower side is not getting recognition at all. It is not the business of the chairman (umpire) in this relay contest to "even things up" by making decisions that are obviously unfair, that is, by recognizing persons as having risen and addressed the Chair first when obviously they were not first.

Any chairman will make mistakes just as professional umpires make mistakes. This fact, however, only makes it the more important that the chairman make no mistakes intentionally.

Debate would be proper participation in a parliamentary manner, but debate is not permitted in this *relay contest* simply because the purpose of the contest is to test each student's facility in making motions rather than in debate.

For the following sample *relay contest* have two rows of eight students each. Let Row One be the A group and Row Two the B group. The teacher should serve as chairman for this first contest. A student chairman should be used, however, just as soon as possible.

RELAY CONTEST DEMONSTRATION

Chairman:—"THE MEETING WILL COME TO ORDER. IS THERE ANY BUSINESS?"

Mr. A-1:—"MR. CHAIRMAN."

Chairman:—"MR. A-1."

Mr. A-1:—"I MOVE THAT WE HAVE A PICNIC."

Someone calls out, "I SECOND THE MOTION."

Chairman:—"IT IS MOVED AND SECONDED THAT WE HAVE A PICNIC. IS THERE ANY DISCUSSION?"

Mr. B-1:—"MR. CHAIRMAN."
Also Mr. A-2 a second later:—"MR. CHAIRMAN."

Chairman:—"MR. B-1."

Mr. B-1:—"I MOVE THAT WE AMEND THIS MOTION BY ADDING THE WORDS 'FRIDAY AFTERNOON'."

Someone calls out, "I SECOND THE MOTION."

Chairman:—"IT IS MOVED AND SECONDED THAT WE AMEND THE MOTION BY ADDING THE WORDS, 'FRIDAY AFTERNOON,' SO THAT THE MOTION, IF AMENDED, WILL READ 'THAT WE HAVE A PICNIC FRIDAY AFTERNOON.' IS THERE ANY DISCUSSION ON THE AMENDMENT?"

Mr. B-2:—"MR. CHAIRMAN." Also Mr. A-2 a second later:— "MR. CHAIRMAN."

Chairman:—"MR. B-2."

Mr. B-2:—"I MOVE THAT WE REFER THIS WHOLE PROPOSITION TO THE ENTERTAINMENT COMMITTEE."
Someone calls out, "I SECOND THE MOTION."

Chairman:—"IT IS MOVED AND SECONDED THAT WE REFER THIS WHOLE PROPOSITION TO THE ENTERTAINMENT COMMITTEE. IS THERE ANY DISCUSSION ON THE MOTION TO REFER?"

Mr. A-2:—"MR. CHAIRMAN."

Chairman:—"MR. A-2."

Mr. A-2:—"I MOVE THAT WE CLOSE DEBATE AND VOTE IMMEDIATELY ON THE PENDING QUESTION."

Someone calls out, "I SECOND THE MOTION."

Chairman:—"IT IS MOVED AND SECONDED THAT WE CLOSE DEBATE AND VOTE IMMEDIATELY ON THE PENDING QUESTION. THE IMMEDIATELY PENDING QUESTION IS THE MOTION TO REFER. THOSE IN FAVOR OF THE MOTION TO CLOSE DEBATE SAY 'I'." *(All vote "I".)* "THOSE OPPOSED SAY 'NO'." *(None vote "No".)*

Mr. A-3 and Mr. B-3:—"MR. CHAIRMAN." "MR. CHAIRMAN."

Chairman ignores both of them and says:— "THE 'I's' HAVE IT BY A TWO-THIRDS VOTE AND THE MOTION TO CLOSE DEBATE IS CARRIED. THE NEXT BUSINESS IS THE VOTE ON THE MOTION TO REFER. THOSE IN FAVOR OF REFERRING THIS PICNIC PROPOSITION TO THE ENTERTAINMENT COMMITTEE SAY 'I'." *(Many vote "I".)* "THOSE OPPOSED SAY 'NO'." *(A few vote "No".)*

Chairman:—"THE 'I's' HAVE IT AND THE MOTION TO REFER IS CARRIED. THE PICNIC PROPOSITION WILL BE REFERRED TO THE ENTERTAINMENT COMMITTEE. IS THERE ANY FURTHER BUSINESS?"

Mr. A-3:—"MR. CHAIRMAN."

Chairman:—"MR. A-3."

Mr. A-3:—"I MOVE THAT WE HAVE A DANCE SATURDAY NIGHT."

Someone calls out, "I SECOND THE MOTION."

Chairman:—"IT IS MOVED AND SECONDED THAT WE HAVE A DANCE SATURDAY NIGHT. IS THERE ANY DISCUSSION?"

Mr. A-4:—"MR. CHAIRMAN."
Also Mr. B-3 a second later:—"MR. CHAIRMAN."

Chairman:—"MR. A-4."

Mr. A-4:—"I MOVE THAT WE AMEND THE MOTION BY ADDING THE WORDS 'IN THE GYMNASIUM'."

Someone calls out, "I SECOND THE MOTION."

Chairman:—"IT IS MOVED AND SECONDED THAT WE AMEND THE MOTION BY ADDING THE WORDS 'IN THE GYMNASIUM' SO THAT THE MOTION, IF AMENDED, WILL READ 'THAT WE HAVE A DANCE SATURDAY NIGHT IN THE GYMNASIUM.' IS THERE ANY DISCUSSION ON THE AMENDMENT?"

Mr. A-5:—"MR. CHAIRMAN."

Chairman:—"MR. A-5."

Mr. A-5:—"I MOVE THAT WE CLOSE DEBATE."

Someone calls out, "I SECOND THE MOTION."

Chairman:—"IT IS MOVED AND SECONDED THAT WE CLOSE DEBATE AND VOTE IMMEDIATELY ON THE PENDING QUESTION WHICH IS THE AMENDMENT. THOSE IN FAVOR OF CLOSING DEBATE SAY 'I'." *(All vote "I".)* "THOSE OPPOSED SAY 'NO'." *(None vote "No.")*

Chairman:—"THE 'I's' HAVE IT BY A TWO-THIRDS VOTE AND THE MOTION TO CLOSE DEBATE IS CARRIED. THE NEXT BUSINESS IS THE VOTE ON THE AMENDMENT THAT WE ADD THE WORDS 'IN THE GYMNASIUM.' THOSE IN FAVOR OF THE AMENDMENT SAY 'I'." *(Many vote "I".)* "THOSE OPPOSED SAY 'NO'." *(A few vote "No".)*

Chairman:—"THE 'I's' HAVE IT AND THE AMENDMENT IS CARRIED. IS THERE ANY DISCUSSION ON THE MOTION AS AMENDED WHICH IS THAT WE HAVE A DANCE SATURDAY NIGHT IN THE GYMNASIUM?"

Mr. B-3:—"MR. CHAIRMAN." Also Mr. A-6 a second later:—"MR. CHAIRMAN."

Chairman:—"MR. B-3."

Mr. B-3:—"I MOVE THAT WE LAY THIS MOTION ON THE TABLE."

Someone calls out, "I SECOND THE MOTION."

Chairman:—"IT IS MOVED AND SECONDED THAT WE TABLE THE MOTION AS AMENDED. THOSE IN FAVOR OF TABLING THE MOTION AS AMENDED SAY 'I'." *(A few vote "I".)* "THOSE OPPOSED SAY 'NO'." *(Many vote "No".)*

Chairman:—"THE 'NOES' HAVE IT AND THE MOTION TO 'TABLE' IS LOST. IS THERE ANY FURTHER DISCUSSION ON THE MOTION AS AMENDED?"

Mr. A-6:—"MR. CHAIRMAN."

Chairman:—"MR. A-6."

Mr. A-6:—"I MOVE THAT WE POSTPONE CONSIDERATION OF THIS MOTION TILL THE NEXT MEETING."

Someone calls out, "I SECOND THE MOTION."

Chairman:—"IT IS MOVED AND SECONDED THAT WE POSTPONE CONSIDERATION OF THIS MOTION AS AMENDED TILL THE NEXT MEETING. IS THERE ANY DISCUSSION AS TO THE ADVISABILITY OF POSTPONEMENT?"

Mr. A-7:—"MR. CHAIRMAN," also Mr. B-4 a second later:— "MR. CHAIRMAN."

Chairman:—"MR. A-7."

Mr. A-7:—"I MOVE THAT WE ADJOURN."

Someone calls out, "I SECOND THE MOTION."

Chairman:—"IT IS MOVED AND SECONDED THAT WE ADJOURN. THOSE IN FAVOR OF THE MOTION TO ADJOURN SAY 'I'." (A few vote "I".) "THOSE OPPOSED SAY 'NO'." (Many vote "No".)

Chairman:—"THE 'NOES' HAVE IT AND THE MOTION TO ADJOURN IS LOST. IS THERE ANY FURTHER DISCUSSION ON THE MOTION TO POSTPONE CONSIDERATION OF THE MOTION AS AMENDED TILL THE NEXT MEETING?"

Mr. B-4:—"MR. CHAIRMAN." Also Mr. A-8 a second later:— "MR. CHAIRMAN."

Chairman:—"MR. B-4."

Mr. B-4:—"I MOVE THAT WE REFER THIS MOTION TO THE ENTERTAINMENT COMMITTEE."

Chairman:—"YOUR MOTION IS OUT OF ORDER. THE MOTION TO POSTPONE TILL THE NEXT MEETING IS BEFORE THE HOUSE AND IT DOES NOT YIELD TO THE MOTION TO REFER. IS THERE ANY FURTHER DISCUSSION ON THE MOTION TO POSTPONE TILL THE NEXT MEETING?"

Mr. A-8:—"MR. CHAIRMAN."

Chairman:—"MR. A-8."

Mr. A-8:—"I MOVE THAT WE CLOSE DEBATE AND VOTE IMMEDIATELY ON THE PENDING QUESTION."

Someone calls out, "I SECOND THE MOTION."

Chairman:—"IT IS MOVED AND SECONDED THAT WE CLOSE DEBATE AND VOTE IMMEDIATELY ON THE PENDING QUESTION."

Chairman:—"CONTEST IS OVER. THE 'A' GROUP WINS."

Note:—In case the motion to adjourn is carried in the midst of a contest the chairman declares the meeting adjourned, sounds his gavel, then sounds his gavel again, promptly calls the new meeting to order and asks, "Is there any business?" or announces that the unfinished business of the last meeting is (whatever it is).

After the class has had many relay contests, the rules may be changed to permit counting debate as "proper parliamentary participation" if the instructor desires to give the students practice in speaking from the floor. However, the instructor should not count remarks as "proper participation" unless the remarks are "to the point." In case the remarks are not "to the point" the chairman should say "your remarks are out of order" because they "do not make sense" or "are ridiculous" or "are not about the motion before the assembly."

Students who stutter or have nervous or emotional inhibitions should be placed at the end of the row so that they may have the easiest opportunity to participate in this strenuous contest.

QUICK CALCULATION OF TWO-THIRDS VOTE

Since the motion to close debate requires a two-thirds vote, chairmen are frequently bothered by the mental arithmetic involved in determining quickly whether the "I" vote is two-thirds of the total vote.

The simplest method of doing this is to double the "No" vote. If the "No" vote doubled is more than the "I" vote, then the "I" vote is not two-thirds of the total. Thus if the vote is "I's" 14, "Noes" 8, the "I's" do not have it by a two-thirds vote because twice 8 is 16. On the other hand, if the vote is "I's" 14, "Noes" 7, the "I's" do have it by a two-thirds vote because twice 7 is 14, and therefore, the vote is "I's" two-thirds, "Noes" one-third. Thus the "I's" have it by a two-thirds vote whenever the "I" vote is twice as much or more than twice as much as the "No" vote.

A little drill on this quick method of determining whether a vote is two-thirds will establish the habit of checking it in the easy way and save the chairman much annoyance later on when he does have to decide this matter of a two-thirds vote before a large group and, perhaps, in the midst of much excitement and confusion.

Lesson VI

PLAIN BOWLING CONTEST

The purpose of this contest is to show in a visual and dramatic manner just how one motion takes precedence over another.

In this contest the mover of a motion and the seconder must stand at the front of the room and face the class while holding a placard handed to them by the secretary. This placard contains the name of the motion they have made such as MAIN MOTION, MOTION TO REFER, etc. The first mover and seconder will, of course, hold the placard MAIN MOTION.

If the next motion made is the motion to amend, then this mover and seconder will stand directly in front of the MAIN MOTION sponsors holding the AMENDMENT placard to show that the amendment takes precedence over the main motion and must be voted on before the main motion can be voted on.

On the back side of the AMENDMENT placard should be the words, "AS AMENDED" so that if the amendment is carried the two sponsors of the amendment can step back beside the main motion sponsors and reverse their placard. Thus the four sponsors with their placards will be as follows:

Before Amendment is adopted

MAIN MOTION

AMENDMENT

After Amendment is adopted

MAIN MOTION

AS AMENDED

If a motion is moved and seconded, then an amendment is moved and seconded, and finally the motion to refer is moved, seconded and carried, all three motions are disposed of for the time being, and the four sponsors of the amendment and main motion must go to the "suspense corner." (See diagram of class room below.)

In this contest the class is divided into two groups with the A group having the most members. The teacher serves as chairman. She should have a student serve as secretary and another student serve as sergeant at arms to hand out the placards as they are needed. The point of the contest is for the A group to make a motion and second it and get it adopted as soon as possible so that their two members who sponsored this main motion can sit down, because according to the rules of this contest the two sponsors of any motion cannot sit down until their particular motion is carried. On the other hand if a motion is defeated, (voted down) the two sponsors of that motion are out of the contest, dead, and must go to the deadman's corner like checkers or chess men jumped or captured by the opponent. When the main motion is temporarily disposed of by the motion to refer, to postpone definitely, or to table, the sponsors of the main motion (and of any pending amendment) are not "dead." They are only "in suspense" and, therefore, they must go to the "suspense" corner.

Those in the "deadman's corner" can neither vote nor make other motions. Dead men are dead. But those in the "suspense corner" *can* vote. They can not make other motions because those in the "suspense corner" are still sponsoring motions that have not yet been voted on. As Mr. Dooley said, "When you're up. you're up, and when you're down, you're down. But when you're only half way up you're neither up nor down." The motions (and motion sponsors) in the "suspense corner" are neither up nor down.

Diagram of classroom

A SAMPLE CONTEST

Teacher as Chairman:— Sounds gavel. "THE MEETING WILL PLEASE COME TO ORDER. IS THERE ANY BUSINESS?"

No. 1 of A Group:—"MR. CHAIRMAN."

Chairman:—"NO. 1-A."

No. 1-A:—"I MOVE THAT WE HAVE A PICNIC."

No. 2-A:—"I SECOND THE MOTION."

Chairman:—"IT IS MOVED AND SECONDED THAT WE HAVE A PICNIC. IS THERE ANY DISCUSSION?" *(No. 1-A and No. 2-A go to front of room and face class, holding MAIN MOTION placard given to them by the sergeant at arms.)*

No. 1-B:—"MR. CHAIRMAN."

Chairman:—"NO. 1-B."

No. 1-B:—"I MOVE THAT WE AMEND THE MOTION BY ADDING THE WORDS 'FRIDAY AFTERNOON'."

No. 2-B:—"I SECOND THE MOTION."

Chairman:—"IT IS MOVED AND SECONDED THAT WE AMEND THIS MOTION BY ADDING THE WORDS 'FRIDAY AFTERNOON', SO THAT THE MOTION, IF AMENDED, WILL READ 'THAT WE HAVE A PICNIC FRIDAY AFTERNOON'. IS THERE ANY DISCUSSION ON THE AMENDMENT?" *(No. 1-B and No. 2-B stand in front of No. 1-A and No. 2-A, face the class, and hold the AMENDMENT placard given to them by the sergeant at arms.)*

No. 3-B:—"MR. CHAIRMAN."

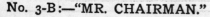

Chairman:—"NO. 3-B."

No. 3-B:—"I MOVE THAT WE ADJOURN."

No. 4-B:—"I SECOND THE MOTION."

Chairman:—"IT IS MOVED AND SECONDED THAT WE ADJOURN. *(Chairman now waits until No. 3-B and No. 4-B get the TO ADJOURN placard from the sergeant at arms and take their place directly in front of No. 1-B and No. 2-B.)*

Then the Chairman continues:— "THOSE IN FAVOR OF ADJOURNMENT SAY 'I'." *(B group all vote "I".)* "THOSE OPPOSED TO ADJOURNMENT SAY 'NO'." *(All of A group vote "No" because, if motion to adjourn is carried, No. 1-A and No. 2-A will have to remain standing until the next meeting since under the rules the sponsors of a motion must remain standing until their motion is voted on.)*

Since the A group is larger than the B group, and all the A group voted against adjournment, the chairman announces as follows:

Chairman:— "THE 'NOES' HAVE IT AND THE MOTION TO ADJOURN IS LOST. NO. 3-B AND NO. 4-B ARE OUT OF THE CONTEST BECAUSE THEIR MOTION WAS DEFEATED. THEY WILL PLEASE GO TO THE 'DEADMAN'S CORNER' AND TAKE NO FURTHER PART IN THIS CONTEST. IS THERE ANY FURTHER DISCUSSION ON THE AMENDMENT?"

After a pause the Chairman says:—"IF NOT, THE VOTE IS ON THE AMENDMENT THAT WE ADD THE WORDS 'FRIDAY AFTERNOON'. THOSE IN FAVOR OF THE AMENDMENT SAY 'I'." *(Let us suppose that Friday afternoon is a satisfactory time for everyone, and, therefore, both A and B groups vote "I".)* "THOSE OPPOSED TO THE AMENDMENT SAY 'NO'." *(No one votes "No".)*

Chairman:—"THE 'I's' HAVE IT AND THE AMENDMENT
IS CARRIED. THE NEXT BUSINESS IS THE MO-
TION AS AMENDED WHICH READS THAT WE
HAVE A PICNIC FRIDAY AFTERNOON. IS THERE
ANY DISCUSSION ON THE MOTION AS AMENDED?"
*(No. 1-B and No. 2-B step back with No. 1-A and No. 2-A
but on their left. No. 1-B and No. 2-B reverse their placard as
they step back beside No. 1-A and No. 2-A. The reverse
side of the Amendment placard reads "AS AMENDED".)*

After a pause the chairman says:—"IF THERE IS NO FUR-
THER DISCUSSION, THE VOTE IS ON THE MOTION
AS AMENDED, WHICH READS THAT WE HAVE A
PICNIC FRIDAY AFTERNOON. THOSE IN FAVOR
OF THE MOTION AS AMENDED SAY 'I'. *(Many vote
'I'.)* THOSE OPPOSED SAY 'NO'." *(Few if any vote
"No".)*

Chairman:—"THE 'I's' HAVE IT AND THE MOTION AS
AMENDED IS CARRIED. THE FOUR SPONSORS OF
THE MOTION AS AMENDED MAY BE SEATED."

Since Group A has succeeded in getting No. 1-A and No.
2-A back in their seats, the contest is over. In bowling you can
not play when there are no pins standing in the alley. Likewise in this parliamentry bowling contest you can not play
when there are no "motion sponsors" before the class.

It is possible to have fourteen or even eighteen sponsors
standing at the front of the room holding their motion placards
provided all of the motions are made in their order of precedence. Thus you could move "to have a picnic," move to amend
by adding the words "at Riverside Park," then move to refer
to the social committee," then move "to postpone consideration
until the next meeting," then move "to close debate," then move
"to table the main motion," and finally move "to adjourn." This
would place fourteen sponsors on the floor at one time. And
this number could have been increased to eighteen by "amending the motion to refer" by adding the words "with instructions
to report at the next meeting," and by "amending the motion to

postpone" by striking out the words "next meeting" and inserting the words "meeting after the next meeting," but each amendment would have had to be moved immediately after the motion to which it applied.

If a motion is moved at the wrong time, (when it is not in order) the mover of that motion is "dead" just as soon as his motion is declared "out of order" and, therefore, the mover of a motion that is "out of order" goes directly to the "deadman's corner" without standing at the front of the room at all. Like a broken pin in a bowling alley, the mover of a motion that is out of order is never permitted to stand in the alley at all.

If the class bell rings in the midst of a bowling contest, the motions before the assembly become "unfinished business," therefore, when the next meeting is called to order by the chairman the sponsors of the "unfinished business" motions must be standing before the assembly just as they were when the class bell rang and "automatically" adjourned the last meeting.

Debate in this contest is limited to two minutes for each side on any one motion.

PRECEDENCE OF AMENDMENTS

Amendments are more complicated than appears at first glance. For instance, the motion to refer takes precedence over an amendment to the main question, but obviously an amendment to the motion to refer must take precedence over the motion to refer. Otherwise it could not be moved while the motion to refer was pending.

The real fact is that amendments have no fixed precedence of their own but take their precedence from the motions to which they apply. The amendment on page 16 is really the "amendment to the main motion." At the bottom of page 15 will be found the "amendment to the motion to refer," and at the bottom of page 14 will be found the "amendment to the motion to postpone to a certain day."

Another confusing situation is that in which someone moves an amendment to the Constitution or to some other motion that has already been adopted. Such an amendment is really a main motion because it does not apply to any pending question, and, like any other main motion, can be moved only when no other business is before the assembly.

APPENDAGE MOTIONS:— A motion that has no fixed precedence of its own but takes its precedence from the motion to which it applies may be called an "appendage motion," since appendages take their rank from the thing or person to which they are appended. The motion to amend and the motion to reconsider (see lesson XI) are both appendage motions.

Lesson VII

MAJORITY — MINORITY CONTEST

Having learned how to handle main motions and the important subsidiary motions, the next step is to change the scheme from the artificial one that has been employed heretofore and operate as a normal assembly with one chairman and many members. For this purpose the class will be divided into two groups, the one to be the Majority with two-thirds of the class as members, and the other to be the Minority with the remainder of the class. A floor leader is appointed for each group although the other members are supposed to assist the floor leader as much as possible.

The contest is as follows:—The majority floor leader makes a motion that is seconded by another member of the majority. When the chairman states the motion and calls for discussion, the majority tries to pass the motion without permitting any amendments. On the other hand, the minority floor leader with the assistance of the other members of the minority attempts to amend the motion, delay action on it, or defeat it. If the majority get their motion passed within five minutes, then the majority wins the contest. If, on the other hand, the minority can change the motion, defeat it, or delay action on it for five minutes, then the minority wins the contest.

A different floor leader should be chosen for each contest so that all can get experience as floor leader. After each contest opportunities should be given for asking questions, because the questions that arise from the actual practice of procedure are always more helpful than those based on a purely academic study of procedure in books.

One rigid rule of this contest is that no motion may be used that has not yet been studied and discussed in class. In the midst of a lively contest is no time to stop for explanation of a new motion.

The following is typical procedure for a majority-minority contest. (In this sample contest it is assumed that there are twenty or more in the majority group and ten or less in the minority group.)

Either the teacher or a student may serve as chairman for this sample contest.

Chairman:—(*sounds gavel*) "THE MEETING WILL COME TO ORDER. IS THERE ANY BUSINESS?"

Majority Floor Leader:—"MR. CHAIRMAN."

Chairman:—"MR. MAJORITY LEADER."

Majority Leader:—"I MOVE THAT WE HAVE A MAS-QUERADE PARTY." Another member of the majority should call out, "I SECOND IT."

Chairman:—"IT IS MOVED AND SECONDED THAT WE HAVE A MASQUERADE PARTY. IS THERE ANY DISCUSSION?"

Minority Floor Leader:—"MR. CHAIRMAN."

Chairman:—"MR. MINORITY LEADER."

Minority Leader:—"I MOVE THAT WE AMEND THIS MOTION BY ADDING THE WORDS 'FRIDAY NIGHT'."

Another minority member calls out, "I SECOND IT."

Chairman:—"IT IS MOVED AND SECONDED THAT WE AMEND THE MOTION BY ADDING THE WORDS 'FRIDAY NIGHT' SO THAT THE MOTION IF AMEND-ED WILL READ 'THAT WE HAVE A MASQUERADE PARTY FRIDAY NIGHT.' IS THERE ANY DISCUS-SION ON THE AMENDMENT?"
(*Both Majority and Minority Leaders should be on their feet addressing the chair.*)

Majority Leader:—"MR. CHAIRMAN." Minority Leader:— "MR. CHAIRMAN."

Chairman:—"MR. MAJORITY LEADER." (*Minority Leader was last one recognized. Chairman should alternate in recognizing each side if members rise on each side at the same time.*)

Majority Leader:—"I MOVE THAT WE CLOSE DEBATE AND VOTE IMMEDIATELY ON THE PENDING QUESTION."

Other majority member calls out, "I SECOND IT."

Chairman:—"IT IS MOVED AND SECONDED THAT WE CLOSE DEBATE AND VOTE IMMEDIATELY ON THE PENDING QUESTION. THOSE IN FAVOR OF THE MOTION TO CLOSE DEBATE SAY 'I'. (*Pause. All majority vote "I".*) "THOSE OPPOSED SAY 'NO'." (*All minority vote "No."*)

Chairman:—"THE VOTE IS 'I's' 20, 'NOES' 10. THE 'I's' HAVE IT BY A TWO-THIRDS VOTE AND THE MO-TION TO CLOSE DEBATE IS CARRIED. THE NEXT BUSINESS IS THE VOTE ON THE AMENDMENT WHICH READS THAT WE ADD THE WORDS 'FRI-DAY NIGHT.' THOSE IN FAVOR OF THE AMEND-MENT SAY 'I'." (*Pause. All the minority vote "I".*) "THOSE OPPOSED SAY 'NO'." (*All the majority vote "No".*)

Chairman:—"THE 'NOES' HAVE IT AND THE AMEND-
MENT IS LOST. IS THERE ANY FURTHER DISCUS-
SION ON THE MOTION TO HAVE A MASQUERADE
PARTY?"

*(Again both the majority and the minority floor leaders arise
and address the chair at the same time.)*

Majority Leader:—"MR. CHAIRMAN." Minority Leader:—
"MR. CHAIRMAN."

Chairman:—"MR. MINORITY LEADER."

Minority Leader:—"I MOVE THAT WE AMEND THE
MOTION BY STRIKING OUT THE WORD 'MAS-
QUERADE' AND INSERTING THE WORD "DINNER'."

Another minority member calls out, "I SECOND IT."

Chairman:—"IT IS MOVED AND SECONDED THAT WE
AMEND THE MOTION BY STRIKING OUT THE
WORD 'MASQUERADE' AND INSERTING THE
WORD 'DINNER,' SO THAT THE MOTION IF
AMENDED WILL READ 'THAT WE HAVE A DIN-
NER PARTY.' IS THERE ANY DISCUSSION ON THE
AMENDMENT?"

Majority Leader:—"MR. CHAIRMAN." Minority Leader:—
"MR. CHAIRMAN."

Chairman:—"MR. MAJORITY LEADER."

Majority Leader:—"I MOVE THAT WE CLOSE DEBATE
AND VOTE IMMEDIATELY ON ALL PENDING
QUESTIONS."

Chairman:—"IS THERE A SECOND?"

Member of majority:—"I SECOND IT."

Chairman:—"IT IS MOVED AND SECONDED THAT WE
CLOSE DEBATE AND VOTE IMMEDIATELY ON ALL
PENDING QUESTIONS. THOSE IN FAVOR OF
CLOSING DEBATE ON ALL PENDING QUESTIONS
SAY 'I'." *(Majority vote "I".)* "THOSE OPPOSED SAY
'NO'." *(Minority vote "No".)*

Chairman:—"THE VOTE IS 'I's' 20, 'NOES' 10. THE 'I's'
HAVE IT BY A TWO-THIRDS VOTE AND THE MO-
TION TO CLOSE DEBATE ON *ALL PENDING QUES-
TIONS* IS CARRIED. THE NEXT BUSINESS IS THE
VOTE ON THE AMENDMENT WHICH READS THAT
WE STRIKE OUT THE WORD 'MASQUERADE' AND
INSERT THE WORD 'DINNER'. THOSE IN FAVOR

OF THE AMENDMENT SAY 'I'." *(Minority vote "I".)* "THOSE OPPOSED SAY 'NO'." *(Majority vote "No".)*

Chairman:—"THE 'NOES' HAVE IT AND THE AMENDMENT IS LOST. THE NEXT ——" *(Interruption).*

Minority Leader interrupts the chairman, "MR. CHAIRMAN."

Chairman permits interruption:—"MR. MINORITY LEADER."

Minority Leader:—"I MOVE THAT WE REFER THIS TO A COMMITTEE."

Chairman:—"YOUR MOTION IS OUT OF ORDER. WHEN THE MOTION TO CLOSE DEBATE HAS BEEN CARRIED IT CUTS OFF THE MOVING OF SUBSIDIARY MOTIONS BELOW IT. THE NEXT BUSINESS IS THE VOTE ON THE MAIN MOTION WHICH READS 'THAT WE HAVE A MASQUERADE PARTY . . . .'" *(Interruption.)*

Another member of the minority party rises and interrupts the chairman, by addressing the Chair:—"MR. CHAIRMAN."

Chairman permits the interruption:—"MR. MINORITY MEMBER."

Minority Member:—"I MOVE THAT WE LAY THE MOTION ON THE TABLE."

Minority Leader:—"I SECOND THE MOTION."

Chairman:—"IT IS MOVED AND SECONDED THAT WE TABLE THIS MOTION. THOSE IN FAVOR OF TABLING THE MAIN MOTION SAY 'I'." *(Minority vote "I".)* "THOSE OPPOSED SAY 'NO'." *(Majority vote "No".)*

Chairman:—"THE 'NOES' HAVE IT AND THE MOTION TO TABLE IS LOST. THE NEXT BUSINESS IS THE VOTE ON THE MOTION TO HAVE A MASQUERADE PARTY. THOSE IN FAVOR OF THIS MOTION SAY 'I'." *(Majority vote "I".)* "THOSE OPPOSED SAY 'NO'." *(Minority vote "No.")*

Minority Leader again attempts to interrupt:—"MR. CHAIRMAN."

Chairman, ignoring the interruption:—"THE 'I's' HAVE IT AND THE MOTION TO HAVE A MASQUERADE PARTY IS CARRIED. IS THERE ANY OTHER BUSINESS?" *(Chairman should not permit interruption during a vote.)*

Majority Leader:—"MR. CHAIRMAN."

Chairman:—"MR. MAJORITY LEADER."

Majority Leader:—"I MOVE THAT WE ADJOURN."

Another majority member calls out:—"I SECOND THE MO-
TION."

Chairman:—"IT IS MOVED AND SECONDED THAT WE
ADJOURN. THOSE IN FAVOR OF ADJOURNMENT
SAY 'I'." (Majority vote "I".) "THOSE OPPOSED SAY
'NO'." (Minority vote "No".)

Chairman:—"THE 'I's' HAVE IT AND THE MOTION TO
ADJOURN IS CARRIED. YOU STAND ADJOURNED."
(Sounds the gavel.)

The Majority win. But they should always win when they
have a two-thirds majority because a two-thirds majority can
always cut off amendments and debate. With debate and amendments cut off, the minority have only a few motions that they can
make, such as "to lay on the table," and "to adjourn." On
the other hand, if the minority have more than one-third of the
vote the minority should always win because the majority cannot
then cut off amendments or debate. For these contests debate
should be limited to one minute for each side on each debatable
motion.

These contests should be continued as long as time will permit with a different set of floor leaders for each contest. When
a student chairman and a student secretary can conduct these contests, the teacher may sit among the students and assist the weak-
er side by quietly making strategic suggestions.

A few alert and articulate students will soon dominate these
majority-minority contests. In order to give the less aggressive
students opportunity to participate the teacher should debar
these alert and overly articulate students from active participation but assign them the task of writing out a detailed criticism
of the procedure and strategy of those who do participate. These
written criticisms of a given majority-minority contest should be
handed to the teacher at the end of the contest so that she can
grade them as to accuracy, completeness, and fairness.

Lesson VIII

MAJORITY-MINORITY BOWLING CONTEST

This type of Bowling Contest is more complete and a little more complicated than the Plain Bowling Contest in lesson six. The B group will attempt to get as many B men in front of No. 1-A and No. 2-A as possible so that it will take the A group some time to knock (vote) these B men out of the way in order that they may vote No. 1-A and No. 2-A back to their seats by voting for the main motion. The Rules are as follows:—

1. The two sponsors of a motion must stand before the class holding the placard for their motion until that motion is adopted, defeated or otherwise disposed of. If the motion is debatable the sponsors must also hold a DEBATABLE placard above the motion placard.

2. When any motion is defeated, the two sponsors of that motion are out of the contest, dead.

3. Any member of the class may vote except those in the "deadman's corner."

4. No motion can be moved unless it is in order, that is, unless it has precedence over the motions already before the assembly. Any person is immediately out of the contest, dead, if he sponsors a motion that is out of order.

5. The A group (the majority group) must get No. 1-A and No. 2-A back to their seats within ten minutes to win.

Chairman:—*(Sounds gavel)* "THE ASSEMBLY WILL PLEASE COME TO ORDER. IS THERE ANY BUSINESS?"

No. 1-A:—"MR. CHAIRMAN."

Chairman:—"No. 1-A."

No. 1-A:—"I MOVE THAT WE HAVE A LITERARY SOCIETY."

No. 2-A:—"I SECOND THE MOTION."

Chairman:—"IT IS MOVED AND SECONDED THAT WE HAVE A LITERARY SOCIETY. IS THERE ANY DISCUSSION?" *(No. 1-A and No. 2-A take the MAIN MOTION placard and stand before the assembly. They also take a DEBATABLE placard to hold above the motion placard.)*

No. 1-B:—"MR. CHAIRMAN."

Chairman:—"NO. 1-B."

No. 1-B:—"I MOVE THAT WE AMEND THE MOTION BY STRIKING OUT THE WORD 'LITERARY' AND INSERTING THE WORD 'DEBATING'."

No. 2-B:—"I SECOND THE MOTION."

Chairman:—"IT IS MOVED AND SECONDED THAT WE AMEND THE MOTION BY STRIKING OUT THE WORD 'LITERARY' AND INSERTING THE WORD 'DEBATING' SO THAT THE MOTION, IF AMENDED, WILL READ THAT WE HAVE A DEBATING SOCIETY. IS THERE ANY DISCUSSION ON THE AMENDMENT?" (*No. 1-B and No. 2-B get the AMENDMENT placard and a DEBATABLE placard*

and stand in front of No. 1-A and No. 2-A. These DEBATABLE placards can be removed by the motion to close debate.)

Note:—The chairman must always hold up the discussion, the vote, or the making of new motions until the sponsors of the last motion moved have secured their motion placard and have taken their proper place in front of the other pending motion (or motions). One of the outstanding duties of a chairman is to prevent confusion in the assembly. Being deliberate is a sign of confidence and strength on the part of the chairman. However, a chairman should not appear to hesitate. Hesitation indicates inability to decide what to do. Be sure of what you are doing, but do it deliberately.

No. 3-B:—"MR. CHAIRMAN."

Chairman:—"NO. 3-B."

No. 3-B:—"I MOVE THAT WE REFER THIS WHOLE SO-
CIETY PROPOSITION
TO A COMMITTEE OF
THREE TO BE AP-
POINTED BY THE
CHAIR."

No. 4-B:—"I SECOND THE
MOTION."

Chairman:—"IT IS MOVED
AND SECONDED THAT
WE REFER THIS
WHOLE SOCIETY PRO-
POSITION TO A COM-
MITTEE OF THREE TO
BE APPOINTED BY THE
CHAIR. IS THERE ANY
DISCUSSION ON THE
MOTION TO REFER?"
*(No. 3-B and No. 4-B get
the TO REFER placard
and a DEBATABLE pla-
card from the sergeant at
arms and stand directly in
front of No. 1-B and No.
2-B.)*

No. 3-A:—"MR. CHAIRMAN."

Chairman:—"NO. 3-A."

No. 3-A:—"I MOVE THAT WE
CLOSE DEBATE AND
VOTE IMMEDIATELY
ON THE PENDING
QUESTION."

No. 4-A:—"I SECOND THE MOTION."

Debatable

MAIN MOTION

Debatable

AMENDMENT

Debatable

TO REFER

---

*Footnote:—The Bowling Contests are not so much contests as
dramatizations. The sponsors of the motions personify the motions they have made. Consequently, the appeal is to the "acting", the make-believe instinct rather than to the competitive
spirit.*

Chairman:—"IT IS MOVED AND SECONDED THAT WE CLOSE DEBATE AND VOTE IMMEDIATELY ON THE PENDING QUESTION." (*No. 3-A and No. 4-A get CLOSE DEBATE placard and stand in front of No. 3-B and No. 4-B.*) "THOSE IN FAVOR OF CLOSING DEBATE SAY 'I'." (*20 vote "I".*) "THOSE OPPOSED SAY 'NO'." (*8 vote "No".*)

Note:—Ordinarily there should be no delay between announcing that the motion to close debate is carried by a two-thirds vote and the putting of the pending motion to a vote. However, in this Bowling Contest there should be long enough delay at this point to permit the sergeant at arms to remove the Debatable placard from the pending motion, or motions, (in this case from the motion to refer) so as to make it absolutely clear that the effect of the adoption of the motion to close debate is to make a motion UN-DEBATABLE that was previously debatable. The fact that you then vote immediately on the pending question follows as a matter of course because if you can not debate a motion then there is nothing else to do but vote on it.

Chairman:—"THE VOTE IS 'I's' 20, 'NOES' 8. THE 'I's' HAVE IT BY A TWO THIRDS VOTE AND THE MOTION TO CLOSE DEBATE ON THE PENDING QUESTION IS CARRIED. THE SERGEANT AT ARMS WILL PLEASE TAKE THE DEBATABLE PLACARD FROM THE MOTION TO REFER. NO. 3-A AND NO. 4-A WILL PLEASE

TAKE THEIR SEATS IN GROUP A. THE NEXT BUSINESS IS THE VOTE ON THE MOTION TO REFER THIS WHOLE SOCIETY PROPOSITION TO A COMMITTEE OF THREE TO BE APPOINTED BY THE CHAIR." *(Interruption.)*

No. 5-B:—"MR. CHAIRMAN."

Chairman permits the interruption:—"NO. 5-B."

No. 5-B:—"I MOVE THAT WE POSTPONE CONSIDERATION OF THIS LITERARY SOCIETY PROPOSITION UNTIL THE NEXT MEETING."

No. 6-B:—"I SECOND THE MOTION."

Chairman:—"YOUR MOTION IS OUT OF ORDER BECAUSE THE VOTE HAS BEEN ORDERED ON THE MOTION TO REFER. THE MOTION 'TO CLOSE DEBATE AND VOTE IMMEDIATELY ON THE PENDING QUESTION' DOES NOT YIELD TO THE MOTION 'TO POSTPONE DEFINITELY.' THEREFORE, NO. 5-B and NO. 6-B ARE OUT OF THE CONTEST AND WILL GO TO THE DEADMAN'S CORNER." *(The chairman should pause here a moment while No. 5-B and No. 6-B go to the deadman's corner. A motion should not be put to a vote while persons are walking about the room except in the case of the motion to adjourn where members have already started to leave the meeting.)* "THE VOTE IS ON THE MOTION TO REFER. THOSE IN FAVOR OF THE MOTION TO REFER SAY 'I'." *(A few vote "I".)* "THOSE OPPOSED SAY 'NO'." *(Many vote "No".)*

Chairman:—"THE 'NOES' HAVE IT AND THE MOTION TO REFER IS LOST. THE SPONSORS OF THE MOTION TO REFER WILL PLEASE GO TO THE DEADMAN'S CORNER. THE NEXT BUSINESS IS THE AMENDMENT THAT WE STRIKE OUT THE WORD 'LITERARY' AND INSERT THE WORD 'DEBATING'. IS THERE ANY DISCUSSION ON THE AMENDMENT?"

No. 7-B:—"MR. CHAIRMAN."

Chairman:—"NO. 7-B."

No. 7-B:—"I MOVE THAT WE LAY THIS WHOLE SOCIETY PROPOSITION ON THE TABLE."

No. 8-B:—"I SECOND THE MOTION."

Debatable

MAIN MOTION

Chairman:—"IT IS MOVED AND SECONDED THAT THIS WHOLE SOCIETY PROPOSITION BE 'TABLED'." *(No. 7-B and No. 8-B get TO TABLE placard and stand in front of the amendment sponsors.)* "THOSE IN FAVOR OF THE MOTION TO TABLE SAY 'I'." *(A few vote "I".)* "THOSE OPPOSED TO THE MOTION TO TABLE SAY 'NO'." *(Many vote "No.")*

Debatable

AMENDMENT

Chairman:— "THE 'NOES' HAVE IT AND THE MOTION TO TABLE IS LOST. NO. 7-B AND NO. 8-B WILL PLEASE GO TO THE DEADMAN'S CORNER. IS THERE ANY FURTHER DISCUSSION ON THE AMENDMENT THAT WE STRIKE OUT THE WORD 'LITERARY' AND INSERT THE WORD 'DEBATING'?"

TO TABLE

No. 5-A:—"MR. CHAIRMAN."

Chairman:—"NO. 5-A."

No. 5-A:—"I MOVE THAT WE CLOSE DEBATE AND VOTE IMMEDIATELY ON ALL PENDING QUESTIONS."

No. 6-A:—"I SECOND THE MOTION."

Chairman:—"IT IS MOVED AN SECONDED THAT WE CLOSE DEBATE AND VOTE IMMEDIATELY ON ALL PENDING QUESTIONS." *(No. 5-A and No. 6-A get CLOSE DEBATE placard and stand in front of amendment sponsors.)* "THOSE IN FAVOR OF CLOSING DEBATE ON ALL PENDING QUESTIONS SAY 'I'." *(16 vote "I".)* "THOSE OPPOSED SAY 'NO'." *(4 vote "No".)*

Chairman:—"THE VOTE IS 'I's' 16, 'NOES' 4. THE 'I's' HAVE IT BY A TWO THIRDS VOTE AND THE MOTION TO CLOSE DEBATE ON ALL PENDING QUESTIONS IS CARRIED. NO. 5-A AND NO. 6-A WILL PLEASE TAKE THEIR SEATS IN GROUP A. THE SERGEANT AT ARMS WILL PLEASE TAKE THE DEBATABLE PLACARDS FROM THE AMENDMENT AND FROM THE MAIN MOTION.

(The Chairman should give the sergeant at arms plenty of time to remove the debatable placards while the assembly can watch him do it so that it will be clear that the motion to close debate on all pending questions removes all the debatable placards no matter how many debatable motions are pending at that time.)

THE NEXT BUSINESS IS THE VOTE ON THE AMENDMENT THAT WE STRIKE OUT THE WORD 'LITERARY' AND INSERT THE WORD 'DEBATING'. THOSE IN FAVOR OF THE AMENDMENT SAY 'I'." *(4 vote "I".)* "THOSE OPPOSED SAY 'NO'." *(16 vote "No".)*

Chairman:— "THE 'NOES' HAVE IT AND THE AMENDMENT IS LOST. NO. 1-B AND NO. 2-B WHO SPONSORED THE AMENDMENT WILL PLEASE GO TO THE DEADMAN'S CORNER. THE NEXT BUSINESS IS THE VOTE ON THE MAIN MOTION THAT WE HAVE A LITERARY SOCIETY. THOSE IN FAVOR OF HAVING A LITERARY SOCIETY SAY 'I'." *(Many vote "I".)* "THOSE OPPOSED SAY 'NO'." *(A very few vote "No".)*

Chairman:—"THE 'I'S' HAVE IT AND THE MOTION TO HAVE A LITERARY SOCIETY IS CARRIED. NO. 1-A AND NO. 2-A WILL PLEASE TAKE THEIR SEATS IN GROUP A."

Note:— The purpose of this contest is, of course, to visualize and dramatize the precedence of motions. As a game the point of the contest is for the B group to keep the sponsors of the main motion standing as long as possible, while the A group attempts to get the sponsors of this main motion back to their seats as quickly as possible. When the B group keeps the sponsors of the main motion from returning to their seats within ten minutes the B group wins the contest.

A motion referred to a committee may, of course, be brought back before the assembly by the committee to which it was referred. A motion postponed for consideration until the next meeting will, of course, be brought before the assembly at the next meeting as a general or special order (see Rule 4 and 5, page 14 in the manual). A motion laid on the table may be "taken from the table" at any time when there is no other business before the assembly. A motion or motions pending when the motion to adjourn is carried become "unfinished business" and must be taken up at the next meeting before any "new business" is in order, but not before committee reports, general orders and special orders. (See Order of Business in manual, page 22.)

Thus to refer, to table, or to postpone consideration of a main motion does not finally dispose of the main motion but it does win the contest for the B group because all the B group undertakes to do in this contest is to prevent the adoption of the main motion for ten minutes. Likewise, an "I" vote on the motion to adjourn does not defeat the main motion, but it does prevent the adoption of the main motion within ten minutes and, therefore, an "I" vote on the motion to adjourn wins the contest for the B group.

When students have learned well how to carry on this contest it can be made even more delightful and alertness provoking by giving the minority one or two more than one third of the membership of the class. This will enable the minority to defeat the motion to close debate until several minority members have been sent to the deadman's corner because the majority voted down their motion.

This contest is excellent for use in demonstrating parliamentary procedure before an adult group. The fact that it is visual and the further fact that each step is delayed while the sponsor and seconder of each motion secure the motion placard and take their proper place at the front of the room make this contest an excellent lesson in procedure for the adult audience, because the adults have time to think out each step before the next motion is moved.

This demonstration may be fitted perfectly into any program so far as time is concerned by the simple device of having one member of the majority serve as time keeper and move to adjourn when the allotted time has expired. The majority should, of course, be told in advance that when this time keeper of theirs moves to adjourn, the majority are to vote "I".

And to make this finish both dramatic and fully informative, the chairman should announce the result of this "I" vote on the motion to adjourn as follows:—

"The 'I's' have it and the motion to adjourn is carried. The pending motions (if any) are 'unfinished business' and will be taken up at the next meeting. You stand adjourned." (Sounds gavel.)

SENIOR MANUAL FOR GROUP LEADERSHIP

AN INSTANT USE GUIDE TO PARLIAMENTARY PROCEDURE

BY

O. GARFIELD JONES

PROFESSOR OF POLITICAL SCIENCE IN THE
UNIVERSITY OF THE CITY OF TOLEDO

NEW YORK

D. APPLETON-CENTURY COMPANY

INCORPORATED

Preface

With one exception this manual contains all the rules in common use governing the discussion and action of groups other than legislative bodies in the United States. The technical rules of procedure used in legislatures are impractical for the ordinary civilian group both because they are quite complicated in order to meet the needs of a large body with a tremendous volume of business and because no two legislatures have exactly the same rules. For instance, on the motion "to table" one set of rules applies in the United States House of Representatives, a different set of rules applies in the Ohio Legislature, and still another set applies in the Legislature of Indiana.

General Henry M. Robert performed a truly great service for the American people when in 1876 he simplified the rules of procedure of the U. S. House of Representatives so as to adapt them to the use of ordinary societies and got this "adaption" accepted generally throughout the United States as the "standard rules of order" for group meetings.

This Senior Manual does not change, nor does it supersede General Robert's splendid "Rules of Order" (except for a minor detail noted below).

This Senior Manual is primarily a pedagogical contribution that enables any ordinary person to use Robert's "Rules" effectively without committing the rules to memory. In fact it has been demonstrated a number of times that seventh grade pupils of average or superior ability can by the use of my "Junior Manual with Lessons" be taught to use the more important motions correctly and with facility after only five lessons of fifty minutes each. And, what is of equal importance, these seventh grade pupils are thrilled by these lessons and exhibit great delight at being able to conduct their group meetings in accordance with standard rules of procedure.

To be sure, the Junior Manual is a simplification of Robert's "Rules," just as Robert's "Rules" were a simplification of congressional procedure. But this simplification has been worked out in such a manner that when these pupils reach the senior high school or college they do not have to unlearn anything before taking up Robert's "Rules" complete, as found in this manual.

The one modification of Robert's "Rules" to be found in the Senior Manual is that the motion "to reconsider and have entered on the minutes for action at the next meeting" is not included in my manual, although the regular motion "to reconsider" is in this manual (page 19). According to Robert's "Rules" the

VII

motion "to reconsider and have entered on the minutes for action at the next meeting" takes precedence over the regular motion "to reconsider" and thus enables two obstreperous members to prevent final action on any motion at one meeting no matter how important.

General Robert recognized this difficulty but suggested that this paralysis of action by two members may be overcome by having the club vote to have a special meeting next day at which time this "special" motion to reconsider may be voted down and the main motion to which it applied be put into effect. But how many organizations are in a position to call a special meeting next day to remove the barrier to final action set up by two contrary members who have paralyzed immediate action by the assembly on a matter of urgent importance to which these two contrary members happen to be opposed? It is my contention that there is less probability of abuse of the regular motion "to reconsider" by the majority than there is probability of the abuse of the motion "to reconsider and have entered on the minutes for action at the next meeting" by any two members of the assembly. Neither Cushing's Manual nor the Rules of Congress recognize any such authority of two members to paralyze the action of the majority. Such authority in the hands of any two members is contrary to the principle of majority rule on which constitutional government is based. It is worse than giving the president an absolute veto because it gives a vital suspensive veto to any two members of the assembly who may be the least responsible and the least intelligent members of that assembly.

The inspiration for working out this manual came from those students and alumni who have demonstrated so clearly the value of this group leadership technique in college life and in adult life generally.

O. GARFIELD JONES.

VIII

FOREWORD

Fundamentally all law is based on custom. Like the common law, parliamentary law is largely based upon the customary practices regulating procedure in group action as developed throughout the centuries. While the fundamental rules are applicable to all group action, a wide difference in detail must necessarily exist when the rules are applied to different groups. For example, the rules of the House of Representatives which afford the basis of most texts on parliamentary law in this country must meet the needs of a body of over four hundred persons meeting daily for months with a great volume of business. Therefore, these rules can not be used in detail by a convention or smaller groups of citizens organized for more or less informal action and convening intermittently.

Technical procedure should be discouraged in legislative bodies and to a greater degree in ordinary parliamentary groups. Rules should be applied and interpreted so as to permit a majority to accomplish its ultimate purpose within a reasonable period of time but only after allowing the minority reasonable opportunity to express its views on the question at issue.

The work of Dr. Jones is unique in its simplicity. The variations from the rules laid down by other texts which he suggests should result in simplifying procedure and should aid in the avoidance of technical complications which are often so irksome to the layman and discourage his interest in parliamentary law. Dr. Jones is making a substantial contribution toward a more effective democracy by his simple application of common sense to procedure in group action.

Lehr Fess

Parliamentarian, House of Representatives,

1919-1927.

INTRODUCTION
Leadership

The effective individual functions through groups, many groups. It is the group that gives him weight in every field of endeavor. Therefore, the effective individual must be effective in groups, that is, he must be a group leader—not necessarily the chairman of the group, but at least the leader of some activity or policy of the group.

Group leadership is an art that anyone can learn, first by learning the rules for group discussion and action called parliamentary procedure, second by practice in the art of leadership. This Group Leadership Manual is designed to provide the rules of procedure for a chairman or a member just as they are needed and without preliminary study. It also provides parliamentary phrases which facilitate practice in the art, the strategy, of group leadership.

The Rules of Parliamentary Procedure are the Basis of Constitutional Government

Democratic government is based absolutely upon the principle of majority rule. But majority rule requires that the minority abide by the will of the majority. And the willingness of the minority to abide by the will of the majority is, in turn, based upon the willingness of the majority to permit the minority to "have their say" before final action is taken. The cry of Themistocles to Eurybiades was "Strike, but hear me!"

As has been said so frequently, the chief purpose of parliamentary procedure is to protect the rights of the minority. The majority can usually take care of itself. In a government controlled by public opinion, which we call a democracy, accepted rules of parliamentary procedure are not only of the highest importance for legislatures, they are the foundation of freedom in every meeting, large or small, throughout the nation.

Good citizenship is a habit of dealing with one's fellow citizens. It is the habit of giving one's best thoughts and efforts for the general welfare but at the same time being willing to consider the thoughts and efforts of others, and, if need be, compromising with or submitting to the thoughts and efforts of the majority of one's fellow citizens. This habit of participation in, compromising with, and submission to the will of the majority may be acquired only as other habits are acquired; by practice, and then more practice.

This Group Leadership Manual is designed to facilitate the development of this type of good citizenship conduct by making it possible for all the groups in the country, be they highly educated or not, to conduct their meetings according to the accepted rules of parliamentary procedure that have been worked out by a thousand years of English and American experience in self-government through deliberative assemblies.

Effective Groups

For a group to be of maximum effectiveness it must have competent leadership and also a high degree of competence among its members. Among other things this implies that the members know how to deliberate and how to crystallize these deliberations into group action. This also implies that the chairman knows how to inspire and direct group discussion and how to facilitate the crystallizing of this discussion into specific group action.

CHAIRMANSHIP

A good chairman is one who inspires confidence by his assurance, and who keeps the assembly informed at all times as to what is before them for consideration and vote. However, no chairman can inspire confidence and maintain the dignity of the assembly when he is making one erroneous decision after another. Correctness is a matter of fact, not a matter of conceit.

This Group Leadership Manual provides instantaneously the facts which enable a competent citizen to be correct in his decisions as chairman or correct in his conduct as an active member of the assembly.

Dignity and leadership are personal qualities that are dependent in part only on being correct. But a citizen with an average amount of personality may, by practice, develop dignity and leadership ability if he is correct and fair in his conduct in the group.

Just as the dictionary enables any literate person to spell correctly when writing a letter, just so does this manual enable any citizen to function in a civic, business, educational or other discussion group either as chairman or as an active member.

Group discussion and group action, like group games, require rules for their operation. The rules for group discussion and group action are commonly called "parliamentary procedure" because they were first worked out into a complete scheme by a thousand years of English and American legislative experience.

However, all the elaborate and detailed rules used by a state or national legislature are not necessary for the conduct of business in a small club or group. All the technical knowledge and experience needed when operating an aeroplane are not needed when operating a motorcycle, less still when operating a tricycle.

It is a waste of time for the ordinary citizen to attempt to master all the formal rules of procedure for conducting business in a group because the detailed rules are too numerous for the human mind to retain and use with facility just as learning to spell all the words in the dictionary is not worth while unless one is contesting for the spelling championship of the United States. For most of us it is sufficient to have the dictionary handy so that we can spell correctly the words we actually use from day to day. The fact is that by the quick use of a dictionary the average man can readily out-spell the expert speller who does not have the use of a dictionary.

In similar manner the average citizen may by the use of this manual more readily and correctly decide points of parliamentary procedure than can the expert parliamentarian who has no such reference manual to use. This is so because the general philosophy of procedure which the expert parliamentarian does know may not always suffice to solve certain technical points that are more arbitrary than philosophical just as the general rules of spelling do not always suffice in determining the spelling of proper names for the simple reason that the spelling of proper names is frequently determined by the arbitrary will of the owner of the name rather than by the general rules of spelling. In short, the average citizen needs to know enough parliamentary procedure to fill satisfactorily the group position in which he finds himself from time to time. To know less is to seriously reduce his efficiency. To know more requires, as a rule, more time than he can devote to the subject.

This Group Leadership Manual has been devised to fill this specific need of the busy citizen. An adult of superior ability can use this manual without any previous study other than to learn the sequence of motions. This sequence must be learned in order that the user of the manual may turn to any motion on the instant. This sequence is not according to alphabetical order. On the contrary, the sequence of motions in this manual is their sequence in rank or precedence. That is to say, any motion indexed on the left hand side takes precedence of those on the right hand side, and any motion on either side takes precedence over the motions that are below it on that side (with certain indicated exceptions). Or, stated conversely, any motion indexed on the right hand side yields to any motion indexed on the left side, and any motion below yields to any motion indexed above it on the same side. Variations from this general rule are clearly indicated under each motion involved in the variation.

CLASSIFICATION AND PRECEDENCE OF MOTIONS

The main motion (page 18) is the main idea or resolution that the assembly is working on, such as, "I move that we have a picnic Friday afternoon." You can have only one such main idea before the assembly at any one time. To have two main but distinct ideas before the assembly at one time would cause endless confusion both in the discussion and in the voting. Therefore, the main motion has the lowest rank or "precedence" of all the motions because a main motion can be moved only when there is nothing else before the assembly.

Now, when a main motion, such as "to have a picnic Friday afternoon" is before the assembly, any of the motions above it (pages 1 to 17) may be moved. That is to say, any member of the assembly may move "to amend the motion by adding the words 'in Sunset Park'," or move "to refer this picnic idea to the entertainment committee," or move "to postpone consideration of this 'picnic' motion until tomorrow," or move "to close debate on this 'picnic' motion," or move "to lay this 'picnic' motion on the table," (that is lay it aside for the present), or "rise for information" and ask if there is to be no school Friday afternoon, or move "to adjourn."

All of these motions take **precedence** over the main motion because they apply to the main motion or, as in the case of the motion to adjourn, they are of such immediate importance to the assembly that they must be voted on at once regardless of what else is before the assembly.

The motion to adjourn is called a "privileged motion" because it is of such importance to the assembly that it must be acted on at once. Suppose the furnace was filling the room with smoke so rapidly that the members of the assembly could hardly breathe. Obviously it would be absurd to remain in the smoke-filled room to continue the discussion on "the picnic." Some member should move **to adjourn.** The chairman would put this to a vote, and if the majority were in favor of adjournment the Chair would declare the assembly adjourned regardless of any other motions that might be before the assembly.

"To rise" to a point of order, or for information, is called an incidental motion, because while it does not apply to the main motion "to have a picnic" it is **incidental to it.** Thus the person who "rose for information" and asked "Is there to be no school Friday afternoon?" wanted to know the answer to this question before he voted on the motion to have a picnic. If there was to be no school, then he was in favor of the picnic, but if there was to be school he was not in favor of having the picnic. A person might

XIII

rise to a point of order and then tell the Chair that there was too much noise in the room.

This "incidental" motion has precedence over the main motion because the member wants his question answered before the vote is taken on the "motion to have a picnic Friday afternoon" or wants the assembly to be more quiet so he can hear the discussion.

Thus it is easy to see why the motion "to adjourn" and "rising to a point of order" or "for information" are permitted to interrupt other business and must be acted on at once.

The motions (12 to 17) that apply to the main motion and take precedence over it are called subsidiary motions because they are "subsidiary to the main motion." They have no purpose in themselves. Their only purpose is to affect the main motion. Thus the purpose of the motion to amend is to change the main motion; the motion to refer, the motion to postpone consideration, and the motion to table all serve to dispose of the main motion temporarily, while the motion to close debate, if passed by a two-thirds vote, cuts off any further discussion.

Thus we have the four classes of motions: privileged, (pages 1 to 4), incidental, (pages 5 to 11), subsidiary, (pages 12 to 17), and main, (page 18). These motions are arranged in the manual according to their rank or precedence, the one of lowest rank at the bottom (page 18) and the one of the highest rank at the top (page 1). And this ranking is absolute (with a few exceptions to be explained later) so that any motion can be moved when a motion below it in precedence is before the assembly. Conversely, no motion can be moved if a motion above it in precedence is before the assembly. Thus if someone moved that we have a picnic Friday afternoon, and someone else moved that this motion "be referred to the entertainment committee," then the motion to "amend the main motion by adding the words 'Sunset Park'" would be **"out of order"** because the motion to refer does not yield to the motion to amend, or, conversely the motion to amend does not take precedence over the motion to refer.

Of course, if the motion to refer is voted down, then the motion to amend may be used because then the motion to refer is no longer before the assembly; it has been disposed of by a negative vote.

On the other hand it is possible to have seven motions before the assembly at one time provided they are made in the right sequence; that is, if a main motion was moved, then an amendment to that motion, then the motion to refer, then the motion to postpone consideration until tomorrow, then the motion to close debate, then the motion to lay on the table, then a point of order was raised, and finally it was moved to adjourn. (The point of order would be decided by the Chair as soon as it was raised, consequently, it would not be pending when the motion to adjourn was moved.)

Continued to Back of Manual, Page XV

Member:—"Mr. Chairman" (Pause for recognition) "I move that when this assembly adjourns, it adjourn to meet (state the time) in (name the place, if necessary)".

Chairman:—"It is moved and seconded that when this assembly adjourns, it adjourn to meet (state the time) (and if necessary, the place). Is there any discussion?" (See 4, opposite page.)

Put to VOTE:—"The vote is on the motion that when this assembly adjourns, it adjourn to meet (state time and place). Those in favor of fixing the time for the next meeting at (state time and place) say 'I'. (Pause) Those opposed say 'No'."

"I" vote:—"The 'I's' have it and the motion fixing the time for the next meeting is carried. The next meeting will be held at (state time and place). Is there any other business?" (Consult secretary as to next business.)

"No" vote:—"The 'Noes' have it and the motion to fix the time for the next meeting is lost. Is there any other business?" (Consult secretary.)

1	2	3	4
May apply to the following motions	May interrupt a member who has the floor.	Mover must first be recognized	Requires a second
None	No	Yes	Yes

Note:—Ordinarily, the motion to fix the time for the next meeting is just a main motion such as "I move that the next meeting be at seven thirty, next Wednesday night instead of the usual time, eight-thirty." This motion has no privilege because there will be a meeting next Wednesday at eight-thirty even though the above motion is never moved, or, having been moved, is defeated.

But, if there is no time fixed for the next meeting, the motion to adjourn puts an end not only to this meeting but also to any future meetings. Consequently, when no time is fixed for the next meeting, the motion "to fix the time for the next meeting" is the most highly privileged of all motions and can be moved even after the motion to adjourn has been moved, seconded and voted on, provided the chair has not yet declared the meeting adjourned. Of course the meeting is over and no further business can

1. When privileged (see 6) takes precedence of all other motions except a motion to recess already pending.

2. Is in order even after a vote to adjourn if the result of the vote has not yet been announced by the chair.

3. May be amended, but only by altering the time or place (or both) at which meeting shall be held.

4. Not debatable when another motion is before the assembly.

5. Not subject to subsidiary motions except amendment. (See 3)

6. Has no privilege when time has already been fixed for next regular meeting.

5	6	7	8
Debatable	Vote required	May be renewed	Motions that may apply to it
Not when privileged (See 4 and 6)	Majority	Not for same time	Amend, reconsider

be transacted once the Chair, if properly authorized, declares the meeting adjourned.

However, when there is need for another meeting, or when there is necessity for changing the time of the next meeting, the Chair should call attention to this necessity if the motion to adjourn is moved before the time for the next meeting has been determined.

When no time has been fixed for the next meeting, the motion to adjourn is not privileged (see rules on "to adjourn" page 2) and therefore, is not in order when any other motion is pending. In short, the motion to adjourn is just an ordinary main motion when no time has been fixed for the next meeting.

The general belief that the motion to adjourn is "always in order and not debatable" is based on the fact that in nearly all organizations the time is fixed for the next meeting and therefore, the motion to adjourn is highly privileged and is not debatable.

Member:—"Mr. Chairman" (Pause for recognition) "I move that we adjourn."

Chairman:—"It is moved and seconded that we adjourn. Those in favor of adjournment say 'I.' (Pause) Those opposed say 'No'."

"I" vote:—"The 'I's' have it and the motion to adjourn is carried. You stand adjourned." (Sound gavel.)

"No" vote:—"The 'Noes' have it and the motion to adjourn is lost. The next business is (consult secretary)."
Or, Is there further discussion on (state motion before assembly when it was moved to adjourn).

1	2	3	4
May apply to the following motions	May interrupt a member who has the floor.	Mover must first be recognized	Requires a second
None	No	Yes	Yes

IN COMMITTEE:—When a committee finishes its business it should "rise" or "rise and report." However, a committee may "adjourn" from time to time till its business is completed.

1. When unqualified, takes precedence of all motions except to fix time for next meeting.
2. When qualified, it is without privilege.
3. Is in order even after vote ordered on main question.
4. Debatable only when not privileged (see 7), or when adjournment would constitute a dissolution of the assembly.
5. Renewable, but only after some progress.
6. A special order fixing the time for adjournment takes precedence over everything. But this special order may be postponed by a two-thirds vote.
7. Not privileged when no time has been fixed for next meeting.
8. Not debatable when privileged.
9. Cannot be reconsidered, amended or have any other subsidiary motion applied to it if it is unqualified.
10. Quorum is not required for its adoption.
11. It is not always in order. May not interrupt a speaker or the verification of a vote; may not be entertained during a division, nor be renewed until some progress has been made.

5	6	7	8
Debatable	Vote required	May be renewed	Motions that may apply to it
Not when privileged	Majority (See 10)	Yes, after progress	None

TO RECESS:—A motion to Recess for a short period has no precedence unless proposed as an urgent question of privilege. (See Question of Privilege, Page 3.)

Member:—"Mr. Chairman" (Pause for recognition) "I move that we recess (state time of recess or duration)." Note:—It is also advisable to state reasons for having a recess.

The rules are the same as "To Adjourn." When the time for the Recess has expired, the Chair again calls the meeting to order and resumes the business of the meeting that was pending (if any) when the Recess began.

Member:—"Mr. Chairman, I rise to a question of privilege."

Chairman:—"Please state your question."

Member:—"I request that the speaker be asked to go to the front of the room so all can hear him."

Chairman:—"Your privilege is granted. Will the speaker please come to the front of the room?"

Question of Privilege and Privileged Motion

Member:—"I rise to a question of privilege."

Chairman:—"Please state your question."

Member:—"As a question of privilege I move that the visitors be asked to leave the room till this business is concluded."

Chairman:—"Your privilege is granted. As a question of privilege it has been moved and seconded that the visitors be asked to leave the room till this business is concluded. Is there any discussion on this privileged motion? etc."

1	2	3	4
May apply to the following motions	May interrupt a member who has the floor.	Mover must first be recognized	Requires a second
None	Yes, if necessary	No	No

PRIVILEGED MOTION resulting from a Question of Privilege.

Chairman:—"It is moved and seconded that (state motion that was given privileged status under Question of Privilege). Is there any discussion on this privileged motion?"

Put to VOTE:—(Same as any other motion.)

"I" vote:—"The 'I's' have it and the privileged motion is carried. (Chairman should take whatever action is required by the adoption of this privileged motion.) Then chairman should go immediately back to the pending question, be it the main motion, or a subsidiary motion."

"No" vote:—"The 'Noes' have it and the privileged motion is lost. Is there further discussion on the (state the question or motion that was pending when the Question of Privilege was raised)."

1. Takes precedence of all other motions except to adjourn and to fix time of next meeting.

2. Questions of privilege (of the first class) that affect the honor, dignity or safety of the assembly are superior to those (of the second class) that concern only individuals. See below.

3. May interrupt a speaker if immediate action is required.

4. Are decided by the Chair subject to appeal to the assembly.

5. May be disposed of by any subsidiary motion, but such subsidiary motion affects only the question of privilege or the resulting privileged motion, not the main question.

6. Final action need not be taken at once.

7. Chair decides only whether question is one of privilege;—not, usually, as to the particular action required. If question is decided to be a question of privilege (by the Chair or by the assembly on appeal), it has then acquired the status of a privileged motion, but see rule 6 above.

Chart for **Questions of Privilege, NOT** resulting Privileged Motions.

5	6	7	8
Debatable	Vote required	May be renewed	Motions that may apply to it
No, but a resulting motion is	Decided by Chair (See 4)	After progress	None apply to question of privilege, but all may apply to resulting privileged motion.

EXAMPLES:—Questions of privilege of first class involve disorder in the gallery, tampering with papers, bad heating or ventilating, etc.

Questions of privilege of second class involve personal threats or attacks, illness, desire to be excused, etc.

Member:—"Mr. Chairman, I call for the order of the day."

Chairman:—"If there is no objection, the order of the day will now be taken up." (Secretary has record of the orders.)

(If called for at the proper time, a special order must be taken up unless there is objection in the form of a two-thirds vote in favor of postponement.)

To Postpone a Special Order

Member:—"Mr. Chairman," (Pause for recognition) "I move that we postpone this special order till the business now before the assembly is concluded (or 'for twenty minutes' or 'till the next meeting')."

Chairman:—(if motion is seconded), **"It is moved and seconded that we postpone this special order until the business now before the assembly is concluded. Those in favor of postponement say 'I.' (Pause) Those opposed say 'No'."**

"I" vote:—**"The 'I's' have it by a two-thirds vote and the special order is postponed until the business now before the assembly is concluded. Is there any further discussion on the motion** (state the motion already before the assembly when the order of the day was called for)?"

"No" vote:—**"The 'Noes' have it by more than a one-third vote and the motion to postpone the special order is lost. The next business is the special order for today at this time** (state the motion or business that was made the special order for this time).

To Call for Order of the Day

1	2	3	4
May apply to the following motions	May interrupt a member who has the floor	Mover must first be recognized	Requires a second
Any special or general order.	Yes, to call for a special order. (See 2 and 11)	No	No

1. Takes precedence of all other motions except adjourn and questions of privilege.

2. May interrupt a speaker to call for a special order, but not for a general order.

3. To be privileged, the call must be for the orders generally, not for any particular one.

4. A general order may be postponed by a majority vote.

5. A special order may be postponed by a two-thirds vote.

6. Orders of the Day may be taken up by the Chair without a motion or a vote if no one objects.

7. Does not require a second.

8. Is not debatable or amendable.

9. Motion to take up part of the orders has no privilege.

10. If not taken up at the time specified, the order is nullified.

11. A later special order cannot supercede or interfere with another special order previously assigned.

12. General orders cannot interfere with established rules.

13. A call for the orders cannot be renewed until the pending question is disposed of.

To Call for Order of the Day

5	6	7	8
Debatable	Vote required	May be renewed	Motions that may apply to it
No	None, it takes 2/3 vote to postpone special order.	Yes, but (See 13)	None, except to postpone orders.

Member:——(Rising, but not waiting to be recognized.) "Mr. Chairman, I rise to a point of order."

Chairman:——"State your point of order."

Member:——"The motion just proposed is out of order because there is already a main motion before the assembly."

Chairman:——"Your point is well taken.   The motion last proposed is out of order."

OR——"Your point is not well taken. (If a member speaking was interrupted by this point of order the chairman should tell that member to resume speaking.)   The speaker will please continue."

Rising to a Point of Order, Parliamentary Inquiry, or Information

1	2	3	4
May apply to the following motions	May interrupt a member who has the floor	Mover must first be recognized	Requires a second
Any motion or act	Yes	No	No

Rising to a Parliamentary Inquiry

1. If the Chair cannot answer the inquiry, he may refer it to the parliamentarian or to some member of the assembly.

2. A parliamentary inquiry may not lead to **debate**, nor to an **appeal.**

Member:——"Mr. Chairman, I rise to a parliamentary inquiry."

Chairman:——"State your inquiry."

Member:——"Is it in order to offer an amendment now?"

Chairman:——"It is."

1. May interrupt a speaker, or even a vote if need be.
2. The point of order is decided by the Chair.
   (a) If dissatisfied with the decision of the chair any member may APPEAL to the assembly for a final decision.

   Form of APPEAL:—"I appeal from the decision of the Chair."

   (An appeal requires a second.) (See appeals, page 6.)
3. Chair may briefly state the reasons for his decision.
4. If Chair is in doubt as to the point of order he may refer it to a vote of the assembly for final decision.
5. A member having the floor when point of order is raised, must take his seat until the point of order is decided.
6. A point of order must be raised immediately after the error has been made except in the case of a clear violation of the constitution or by-laws.
7. Does not require a second and is not debatable.
8. No other motion may apply to it.

5	6	7	8
Debatable	Vote required (Point of order only)	May be renewed	Motions that may apply to it
No, but see appeals	None, unless appealed, then majority	No	None but see appeals

Rising for Information

1. All requests for information are addressed to the Chair even though aimed at another member.
2. All answers to questions are addressed to the Chair.
   (a) Direct controversies between members are an affront to the dignity of the assembly.
3. A member rising too often should not be given recognition by the Chair.

Member:—"Mr. Chairman, I rise for information," or "I should like to ask the gentleman a question."

Chairman:—**"State your question."** In second inquiry chairman asks the member speaking from the floor if he is willing to be interrupted. If he is, the chairman then turns to the member who rose for information and says:—**"State your question."** (See 1 and 2 above.)

Member:—"Mr. Chairman, I appeal from the decision of the Chair."

Chairman:—"There is an appeal from the decision of the Chair. (If debatable, Is there any discussion?) Those in favor of sustaining the decision of the Chair say 'I.' (Pause) Those opposed to sustaining the decision of the Chair say 'No'."

"I" vote:—"The 'I's' have it and the decision of the Chair is sustained." (Tell the assembly what is next in order.)

"No" vote:—"The 'Noes' have it and the decision of the Chair is reversed by the vote of the assembly." (Tell the assembly what is next in order under this reversed ruling.)

No Appeal on Questions of Dilatory Motions

"The object of a parliamentary body is action, not stoppage of action." Therefore, the Speaker of the United States House of Representatives has declined to entertain debate or appeal on question as to dilatoriness of a motion, because to do so would be to nullify the rule; but he has recognized that the authority conferred by the rule should not be exercised until the object of the dilatory motion "becomes apparent to the house." Usually, but not always, the Speaker "awaits a point of order from the floor before acting." (Rules of House of Representatives of U. S. 71st Congress, 1929, page 346, section 785.)

1	2	3	4
May apply to the following motions	May interrupt a member who has the floor	Mover must first be recognized	Requires a second
Any decision by the Chair	Yes (See 7)	No	Yes

1. Must be seconded.

2. Takes precedence of the question which gives rise to it.

3. Is in order even when another member has the floor.

4. Yields to adjournment, questions of privilege, and orders of the day.

5. Subject to motion to table and to close debate, if debatable. batable.

   (a) Effect of motion to table in this connection is to "kill the appeal without debate" and thus sustain the decision of the chair without a direct vote on the appeal.

6. A tie vote on an appeal sustains the decision of the Chair.

7. Not in order unless made immediately after decision by the Chair.

8. Not in order when another appeal is pending. (Chair's decisions are final on all points of order raised while an appeal is pending.)

9. Not debatable if made when an undebatable motion is pending.

10. Not debatable if appeal relates only to decorum, to violation of the rules, or to order of business.

11. Cannot be amended.

12. If debate is closed on the appeal or the appeal is tabled, this action does not affect the main motion pending.

5	6	7	8
Debatable	Vote required	May be renewed	Motions that may apply to it
No (See 5, 9, 10)	Majority	No	To lay on table, to close debate. reconsider

Member:—"Mr. Chairman" (Pause for recognition) "I move to suspend the rules which interfere with (specify the items interfered with by present rules).

Chairman:—"It is moved and seconded that we suspend the rules which interfere with (specify items interfered with by rules). Those in favor of suspension of these rules say 'I.' (Pause) Those opposed to suspension of these rules say 'No'."

"I" vote:—"The 'I's' have it by a two-thirds vote and the motion to suspend the rules is carried." (State the next business under suspension of the rules.)

"No" vote:—"The 'Noes' have it by more than a one-third vote and the motion to suspend the rules is lost." (State the next business under the rules.)

1	2	3	4
May apply to the following motions	May interrupt a member who has the floor	Mover must first be recognized	Requires a second
Any motion where needed	No	Yes	Yes

1. Takes precedence of the main motion and all subsidiary motions, but yields to all privileged motions.

2. Requires two-thirds vote unless otherwise specified in the constitution or by-laws.

3. Rules can be suspended **only** when they make provision for such suspension, and then only in accordance with such provisions.

4. The motion to suspend the rules is exhausted on the one purpose specified in the motion.

5. Cannot be debated.

6. Cannot have any subsidiary motion apply to it.

7. Cannot be reconsidered.

8. Cannot be renewed for the same purpose, except at a later meeting.

6	5	7	7
Debatable	Vote required	May be renewed	Motions that may apply to it
No	Usually 2/3 See Constitution	No, except by unanimous consent	None

As a Subsidiary Motion

(To Postpone to Certain Day)

For example:—When Report of Committee on By-Laws is before the Assembly.

Member:—"Mr. Chairman" (Pause for recognition) "I move that we postpone consideration of this report till Friday at 3 P. M. and make it a special order for that time."

Chairman:—"It is moved and seconded that we postpone consideration of the By-Laws Committee Report till Friday at 3 P. M. and make it a special order for that time. Is there any discussion either on the postponement or on making it a special order for that time?" (Requires two-thirds vote.)

Put to VOTE:—"The vote is on the motion to postpone the By-Laws Committee Report till Friday at 3 P. M. and make it a special order for that time. Those in favor say 'I' (Pause) Those opposed say 'No'."

"I" vote:—"The 'I's' have it by a two-thirds vote and the motion is carried to postpone till Friday at 3 P. M. and create a special order for that time. Is there any other business?"

"No" vote:—"The 'Noes' have it by more than a one-third vote and the motion to postpone definitely and create a special order is lost. Is there any further discussion on the Report of the Committee on By-Laws?"

Chart for Motion to Create a Special Order

1	2	3	4
May apply to the following motions	May interrupt a member who has the floor	Mover must first be recognized	Requires a second
Main motion	No	Yes	Yes

To Create General Order

1. Requires majority vote only.
2. Cannot interfere with established rules.
3. In all other ways same as motion to create special orders.

1. May be made as a main motion or as motion to postpone to certain day.

2. Requires two-thirds majority whether as main or subsidiary motion.

3. At the time specified a special order takes precedence of any interfering general order. (See Orders of Day 1, 2, 5, 9 and 11 on page 4R.)

4. Has no privilege over ordinary main motion or motion to postpone to certain day.

As a Main Motion

Member:—"Mr. Chairman" (Pause for recognition) "I move that (the report of the Committee on By-Laws) be made a special order for (Friday at 3 P. M.)."

Chairman:—"It is moved and seconded that (the report of the By-Laws Committee) be made a special order for (Friday at 3 P. M.). Is there any discussion?"

Put to VOTE:—"The vote is on the motion that the (report of the By-Laws Committee) be made a special order for (Friday at 3 P. M.) Those in favor say 'I.' (Pause) Those opposed say 'No'." (Requires two-thirds vote.)

"I" vote:—"The 'I's' have it by a two-thirds vote and the special order is carried. (The report of the By-Laws Committee) will be a special order for (Friday at 3 P. M.). Is there any other business?"

"No" vote:—"The 'Noes' have it by more than a one-third vote and the motion to create a special order is lost. Is there any other business?"

5	6	7	8
Debatable	Vote required	May be renewed	Motions that may apply to it
Yes	2/3	After progress	All

Orders of the day once created have status of established rules and, therefore, can be changed only by a two-thirds vote same as "suspension of rules."

Chair should bring up motions (ordered by motion to create general or special orders) at the time ordered. If he fails to do so, any member may "call for orders of the day." (See motion "to call for orders of the day" page 4.)

To Withdraw A Motion

Member:—who made the original motion—"Mr. Chairman" (Pause for recognition) "I desire to withdraw my motion."

Chairman:—"Mr. X asks leave to withdraw his motion. If there is no objection, the motion will be withdrawn. Is there any other business?"

If any member objects to the withdrawal, some other member should rise, be recognized, and move:—

Other Member:—"Mr. Chairman" (Pause for recognition) "I move that Mr. X be allowed to withdraw his motion."

Chairman:—"It is moved that Mr. X be allowed to withdraw his motion. Those in favor say 'I.' (Pause) Those opposed say 'No'."

"I" vote:—"The 'I's' have it and Mr. X has permission to withdraw his motion. Is there any other business?"

"No" vote:—"The 'Noes' have it and permission to withdraw the motion before the assembly is denied. Is there any further discussion on Mr. X's motion that we (state the motion)."

Chart of Motion to Permit Withdrawal of a Motion

1	2	3	4
May apply to the following motions	May interrupt a member who has the floor	Mover must first be recognized	Requires a second
Any motion	No	Yes	No

TO RENEW A MOTION (There is no "motion to renew a motion").

a. A main question cannot be renewed except by motion to reconsider or to take from the table.

b. An amendment cannot be renewed in the same form if objection is made except by the motion to reconsider.

1. A main motion may be withdrawn (by the mover) at any time before final action is reached, provided no one objects.

2. If objection is made, leave to withdraw may be granted by a motion to that effect moved by another member.

3. Cannot be debated or amended.

Chart of Motion to Permit Withdrawal of a Motion

5	6	7	8
Debatable	Vote required	May be renewed	Motions that may apply to it
No	Majority	After progress	Reconsider

TO RENEW A MOTION

1. Any privileged motion, any incidental motion except objection to consideration and suspension of the rules for an incidental purpose, and any subsidiary motion except a specific amendment (see b, opposite page) may be renewed after progress in business has altered the former state of affairs.

The usual method of voting is by **sound** (called viva voce voting). This is quick, convenient, but not accurate for a close vote.

A **show of hands** is likewise quick and convenient, but not accurate for a close vote.

CALLING FOR A DIVISION.   After a vote by **sound** (or, in a large assembly by **show of hands**) any member may "call for a division" of vote, that is, a vote that can be accurately counted: rising vote, roll call or an actual "division."

Member:—"Mr. Chairman, I call for a division!"   Or, without rising the member may simply call out "DIVISION!"

Chairman:—"A division is called for. Those in favor of the motion please stand. (After counting) Be seated. Those opposed please stand. (After counting) Be seated."

If the chairman himself is in doubt as to an "I" and "No" vote he should say, **"The Chair is in doubt. Those in favor of this motion please rise** (or raise the right hand)" etc.

"AYE" vs. "I"—In this Manual the adverb meaning "yes" is spelled "I" as Shakespeare spelled it. Common usage is to spell it "aye," and pronounce it "I" but this leads to confusion because "aye" meaning "forever" is pronounced "A." By spelling it "I" there is neither confusion as to pronunciation nor as to meaning. This voting "I" may either be taken as the adverb meaning "yes," or as an abbreviated form of "I am in favor of it" or "I vote for it."

Rules

1. Vote by ballot may be ordered by a motion to that effect, provided it is not already required by the Constitution or By-Laws.

2. Motion to ballot (or vote by roll call) is not debatable.

3. When balloting is ordered, Chair should appoint two or more tellers to conduct the vote by distributing, collecting and counting the ballots.

Member:—"Mr. Chairman" (Pause for recognition) "I move that the vote on this question be by ballot."

Chairman:—"It is moved and seconded that the vote on this question be by ballot. Those in favor of voting by ballot say "I." (Pause) Those opposed to voting by ballot say 'No'."

"I" vote:—"The 'I's' have it and the motion to ballot is carried. I appoint Mr.——, Mr. —— and Mr.—— as tellers to distribute, collect and count the ballots."

"No" vote:—"The 'Noes' have it and the motion to vote by ballot is lost. The next business is (whatever motion is immediately pending)." (Consult secretary if in doubt.)

Tellers Report:—The tellers should hand to the secretary a written tabulation of the vote just as soon as possible.

Member:—(Rising, but not waiting to be recognized) "Mr. Chairman, I object to the consideration of this motion!"

NOTE:—(Never put a motion in negative form.)

Chairman:—"There is objection to the consideration of this motion. Those in favor of considering this motion say 'I'. (Pause) Those opposed to considering this motion say 'No'."

"I" vote:—"The 'I's' have it by more than a one-third vote and the motion will be considered. Is there any discussion on the motion that we (state the original motion). (Go to page 18, left, **Put To VOTE** phrase next.)

"No" vote:—"The 'Noes' have it by a two-thirds vote and the motion that we (state original motion) will not be considered. Is there any other business?"

1	2	3	4
May apply to the following motions	May interrupt a member who has the floor	Mover must first be recognized	Requires a second.
Main question, and questions of privilege	Yes	No	No

1. Applies only to main motion and to questions of privilege.

2. Is in order only when question is first introduced and before debate.

3. May interrupt a member speaking.

4. Requires a two-thirds vote in the negative (two-thirds vote against consideration).

5. Chairman himself may raise the question of consideration.

6. Requires no second.

7. Cannot be debated or amended.

8. If more than one-third of assembly votes in favor of consideration, then the motion to lay on the table is not immediately in order.

5	6	7	8
Debatable	Vote required	May be renewed	Motions that may apply to it
No	2/3 in negative	No	Reconsider

INDEX

INDEX (Cont'd)

a.   Chairman:—(Sounds gavel) **"The meeting will come to order."** (When members have become quiet) **"The secretary will read the minutes of the last meeting."** Or, (Business is now in order).

    (After reading of the minutes)

b.   Chairman:—**"Are there any objections to or corrections of the minutes?"** (Pause) **"If not, the minutes will stand approved as read. The next business is ——."**

    (If minutes are corrected):—**"If there are no further corrections, the minutes will stand approved as corrected. The next business is ——."**

    (If there is disagreement in the assembly as to a certain correction, this point of correction should be put to a vote of the assembly to settle it officially).

c.   ORDERS OF THE DAY. (See pages 4 and 8.)
    (If, for example, the report of the finance committee had been made a special order for this meeting):—

Chairman:—**"The report of the finance committee was made a special order for this meeting. The chairman of the finance committee will read his report."** (See 5, opposite page for handling reports and committee recommendations.)

d.   ADJOURNMENT. Chairman:—**"If there is no further business, a motion to adjourn is in order."** (See page 2.)

    (If adjournment has been previously ordered at a set time, say at ten P. M., the Chair adjourns the meeting automatically at the time specified.)

Chairman:—**"It is now ten o'clock. You stand adjourned."**
    (Chairman sounds gavel and the meeting is ended.)

Each organization has the right to determine whether it shall have any fixed order of business, and, if so, what that order shall be.

Usual Order of Business

1. Calling meeting to order. (See a, opposite page)

2. Reading and approval of minutes. (See b, opposite page)

3. Orders of the day, if any. (See c, opposite page, also pages 4 and 20.)
   a. Special orders. (See pages 4 and 8.)
   b. General orders. (See pages 13 and 20.)

4. Unfinished business. (See minutes of last meeting.)

5. Reports of committees.
   a. Standing committees.
   b. Special committees. (See pages 13 and 8.)

   (The motion "to accept the report" should be made by a person not on the committee. If, however, the report recommends certain action by the entire organization, the chairman of the committee should make the necessary motion immediately after reading the report that recommends such action.)

6. New Business.

7. Adjournment. (However, the motion to adjourn is almost always in order.)

Voting by Chairman:—A chairman who is at the same time a member in full standing can vote on any motion. He can even speak on any motion by asking someone to preside while he takes the floor.

The Vice-President of the United States can not vote on every motion because he is not a senator. He can vote in case of a tie because the Constitution gives him that special privilege.

A wise chairman does not vote when his vote would not be decisive simply because as the umpire of the contest between the proponents and the opponents his task is easier when he refuses to take sides in the controversy.

a. An office must be created by the Constitution or by a motion to that effect before it can be filled by election or otherwise.

b. The Chair must call for nominations.

Chairman:—**"Nominations are now in order for the office of ——."**

c. Nominations do not require a second. However, any number of persons may second a given nomination just to show their support of that nominee.

Member:— **"Mr. Chairman"** (Pause for recognition) **"I nominate Mr. George Smith for president."**

Chairman:—**"Mr. George Smith is nominated. Are there other nominations?"** (After a pause) **"If not, the motion to close nominations is in order."**

d. The motion "to close nominations" is not in order until the assembly is apparently ready to close nominations.

　　1. When there are two or more nominees for the office the motion to close nominations requires a two-thirds vote. (This motion must be seconded.) (See 4, opposite.)

　　2. A negative vote on the motion to close nominations is an obvious criticism of the chairman for putting this motion to a vote too soon.

e. If the Chair recognizes a member and that member moves "that nominations close" (and it is seconded) before ample opportunity has been given for nominations from the floor, the Chair should ignore this premature motion by simply asking, **"Are there further nominations?"** instead of stating the motion "to close nominations." If and when there are no further nominations the Chair may then put the motion "to close nominations" to a vote without waiting for it to be moved a second time.

　　1. The Chair is particularly responsible for protecting the rights of the minority. If the Chair participates in any scheme to "put something over on the assembly," the Chair is guilty of breach of trust. A chairman is pre-
　　　sumed to be honest, fair and politically intelligent.

1. Elections (and nominations) must conform to the procedure (if there be any) prescribed by the Constitution and By-Laws.

2. In case of a tie vote, the election is decided by lot unless the organization adopts a motion to do otherwise.

3. Elections should be by ballot to reduce the personal friction of elections to the minimum.

4. The motion "to close nominations and instruct the secretary to cast a ballot for the nominee" (or a "slate" of nominees) is in order **only** when there is **obviously** no opposition for the office or offices and when ample opportunity has been given for nominations from the floor.

   a. This motion is a legal fiction by which an office is filled "by ballot" without an actual ballot vote by the members of the assembly.

   b. This motion requires a unanimous vote.

Chairman:—**"The 'I's' have it by unanimous vote. Nominations are closed and the secretary is instructed to cast a ballot for the nominee. Mr. —— is declared elected to the office of ——. The next business is ——."** (Consult secretary if in doubt).

"No" vote:—(If any one votes in the negative) **"The 'Noes' have it and the motion to close nominations is lost. Are there any further nominations?"** (Presumably the opponents of this motion will make one or more additional nominations.)

5. The motion "to suspend the rules and elect by acclamation" is in order **only** when the Constitution permits suspension of the election rules. Even when permitted by the Constitution, this procedure usually requires a two-thirds or a three-fourths vote.

6. The motion "to make the vote unanimous" has no legal status, is not "carried" (adopted) if one member objects or votes "No," and can be moved **only** by the candidate next highest in the election just held.

TO RESCIND (or Repeal)

Member:—"Mr. Chairman" (Pause for recognition) "I move that we rescind (or repeal) the motion that (state motion to be rescinded)."

Chairman:—"It is moved and seconded that we rescind the motion that (state motion to be rescinded) Is there any discussion?"

Put to VOTE:—"The vote is on the motion to rescind the motion that (state the motion to be rescinded) Those in favor of the motion to rescind say 'I.' (Pause) Those opposed say 'No'."

"I" vote:—"The 'I's' have it and the motion to rescind is carried. The motion to (state motion to be rescinded) is rescinded. Is there any other business?"

"No" vote:—"The 'Noes' have it and the motion to rescind is lost. Is there any other business?"

1	2	3	4
May apply to the following motions	May interrupt a member who has the floor	Mover must first be recognized	Requires a second
Main motions, appeals, questions of privilege	No	Yes	Yes

To Rescind or Repeal.

1. Is a "specific" main motion.

2. **Not in order when the subject can be reached by "reconsideration."**

3. **Cannot be applied to action that cannot be reversed.**

4. Requires two-thirds vote of members present, or majority vote of entire membership unless previous notice has been given of this particular motion to rescind.

5. Only majority vote of members present is required when notice of this particular motion to rescind was given at the previous meeting, or in the call for this meeting.

5	6	7	8
Debatable	Vote required	May be renewed	Motions that may apply to it
Yes	Majority (See 4 & 5)	Not at same session	All

To Amend the Rules

1. Is a main motion. (See chart for Main Question.)

2. Procedure is usually prescribed in Constitution or By-Laws.

3. Usual practice requires either two-thirds vote at one session or a majority vote in two successive sessions.

Member:—"Mr. Chairman" (Pause for recognition) "I move that we reconsider the vote on the motion (state the motion)."

Chairman:—"It is moved and seconded that we reconsider the vote on the motion (state the motion). (If debatable) Is there any discussion on the motion to reconsider?"

Put to VOTE:—"The vote is on the motion to reconsider the vote on the motion (state the motion to be reconsidered). Those in favor of the motion to reconsider say 'I.' (Pause) Those opposed say 'No'."

"I" vote:—"The 'I's' have it and the motion to reconsider is carried. You now have before you the motion to (state the motion being reconsidered). Is there any discussion on this motion?" (If motion being reconsidered is not debatable it is put to a vote without discussion.)

"No" vote:—"The 'Noes' have it and the motion to reconsider is lost. The next business is (consult secretary as to next business). Or, is there any further business?"

1	2	3	4
May apply to the following motions	May interrupt a the floor member who has	Mover must first be recognized	Requires a second
Any motion except adjourn, suspend rules, lay on table	Yes, for entry (See 3, 4, & 6)	No	Yes

Rules

1. Has high privilege for entry but not (necessarily) for consideration and vote.

2. May interrupt a member who is speaking (for entry, but not for consideration and vote).

3. Must be moved by one who voted with the prevailing side (unless vote was by ballot).

4. For actual consideration and voting its precedence is that of the motion to which it applies.

5. It suspends action on the motion to which it applies until it has been decided.

6. It is in order at the same meeting or during the next succeeding legislative day ONLY after the vote to which it applies was taken.

7. May be applied to all motions except to adjourn, to suspend the rules, or to table.

8. Requires only majority vote in all cases.

9. Has no privilege **for consideration** other than that of the motion to which it applies.

10. Not debatable if motion to which it applies was undebatable.

11. No question can be twice reconsidered.

12. Action that cannot be reversed cannot be reconsidered.

13. Can not reconsider negative vote on motion to postpone indefinitely.

14. Can not reconsider negative vote on a motion that may be renewed "after progress."

5	6	7	8
Debatable	Vote required	May be renewed	Motions that may apply to it
Yes (See 10)	Majority	No	Limit or close debate, lay on table postpone definitely

Member:—"Mr. Chairman," (Pause for recognition) "I move that we," etc.

Chairman:—"It is moved and seconded that we (state the motion). Is there any discussion?"

Put To VOTE:—"The vote is on the motion that we (state the motion). Those in favor of the motion say 'I.' (Pause) Those opposed say 'No'."

"I" vote:—"The 'I's' have it and the motion is carried. Is there any further business?" (Consult secretary.)

"No" vote:—"The 'Noes' have it and the motion is lost. Is there any further business?" (Consult secretary.)

1	2	3	4
May apply to the following motions	May interrupt a member who has the floor.	Mover must first be recognized	Requires a second
No other motion	No	Yes	Yes

Substitute Motion

Member:—"Mr. Chairman," (Pause for recognition) "I move, as a substitute motion, that we (state the substitute motion)."

Chairman:— "It is moved and seconded as a substitute motion that we, (state substitute motion). Is there any further discussion on the original motion, or on the substitute motion?" (At this time either the original motion or the substitute motion or both may be perfected by detailed amendments.) (When there is no amendment pending and no further discussion, the Chair should say)—

Put to VOTE:—"The vote is on the substitution of the last motion for the original motion. Those in favor of the substitution say 'I.' (Pause) Those opposed to the substitution say 'No'."

"I" vote and "No" vote (see other side at bottom of page).

Rules

1. **Takes** precedence of nothing and yields to everything **except** another principal motion offered later.

2. Should be in writing if complicated.

3. May be divided, if advisable, by motion to divide it.

4. Not in order if any other motion is pending.

5. When once decided, a particular main motion cannot be taken up again at that meeting.

5	6	7	8
Debatable	Vote required	May be renewed	Motions that may apply to it
Yes	Majority	Not at same session	All

Rules for Substitute Motion

1. A substitute motion is just an amendment that **changes an** entire sentence or paragraph.

2. It may be amended (like any other amendment).

3. It differs from an amendment only in that the motion to substitute, if adopted, does away entirely with the original motion.

"I" vote:—**"The 'I's' have it and the last motion is substituted for the original motion. Is there further discussion on the motion that was substituted?"** (The vote is next on the adoption of the motion that was substituted, but the form is, of course, the same as though it were the original motion, or the motion as amended. Therefore, go next to **Put To VOTE** phrase above on opposite page.)

"No" vote:—**"The 'Noes' have it and the motion to substitute is lost. Is there any further discussion on the original motion (or the original motion as amended)?"**

Member:—"Mr. Chairman," (Pause for recognition) "I move that we postpone consideration of this motion indefinitely."

Chairman:—"It is moved and seconded that we postpone consideration of this question indefinitely. Is there any discussion on the motion to postpone indefinitely?"

Put to VOTE:—"The vote is on the motion that we postpone consideration of this question indefinitely. Those in favor of the motion to postpone indefinitely say 'I.' (Pause) Those opposed say 'No'."

"I" vote:— 'The 'I's' have it and the motion to postpone indefinitely is carried. Is there any other business?" (Consult secretary.)

"No" vote:—"The 'Noes' have it and the motion to postpone indefinitely is lost. Is there any further discussion on the main question that we (state pending motion)." (Go to page 18, left, **Put to VOTE** phrase next.)

1	2	3	4
May apply to the following motions	May interrupt a member who has the floor.	Mover must first be recognized	Requires a second
Main motion, question of privilege	No	Yes	Yes

Parliamentary Strategy

Note:—When an important matter is unexpectedly brought before the assembly as a main motion it is of great value to the opposition to learn how many members are in favor of this main motion before the main motion comes to a vote. This is accomplished by the opposition moving to postpone indefinitely. This opens the main question to debate (see rule 2) and the opposition then gives their arguments against the main question. When the vote is finally taken on the motion to postpone indefinitely those opposed to the main question will vote for the motion to postpone indefinitely, while those in favor of the main question will vote against the motion to postpone indefinitely.

If the motion to postpone indefinitely is carried, the opposition to the main question are satisfied because the consideration of the question is

Rules

1. Takes precedence of only the main question.

2. Opens main question to debate.

3. Removes subject for the session.

4. Applies only to main question and questions of privilege.

5. Does not yield to amendments.

6. Not subject to subsidiary motions except "close debate."

Parliamentary Strategy:—The only purpose of the motion to postpone indefinitely is to enable the opposition to see how the assembly will vote on the main question without having the main question actually come to a vote. (See note below.)

5	6	7	8
Debatable	Vote required	May be renewed	Motions that may apply to it
Yes	Majority	No	Limit or close debate. Reconsider ("I" vote only)

now indefinitely postponed and can not be brought before the assembly at this session, or at any time this month except by the motion to reconsider.

If the motion to postpone indefinitely is defeated, the chair then asks for discussion on the main question at which time the opposition, seeing that they are outnumbered, can use this opportunity to obstruct to the limit or to compromise. The opposition, having learned the actual strength of those favoring the main question, are now in a position to do whatever they think best. In short, the only purpose of the motion to postpone indefinitely is to check a surprise attack. It is of use **only** to the opposition to the main question.

Member:—"Mr. Chairman," (Pause for recognition) "I move that we amend the motion by (adding, striking out, inserting) the words ———.''

Chairman:—"It is moved and seconded that we amend the motion by (state the amendment), so that the motion, if amended, will read that we (state the motion as it would be changed by the amendment). Is there any discussion on the amendment?"

Put to VOTE:—"The vote is on the amendment that we (state the amendment). Those in favor of the amendment say 'I.' (Pause) Those opposed say 'No'."

"I" vote:—"The 'I's' have it and the amendment is carried. The next business is the motion as amended which reads that we (state motion as amended). Is there any discussion on the motion as amended?" (Go to page 18, left, **Put to VOTE** phrase.)

"No" vote:—"The 'Noes' have it and the amendment is lost. Is there any further discussion on the original motion?" (Go to page 18, left, **Put to VOTE** phrase.)

1	2	3	4
May apply to the following motions	May interrupt a member who has the floor	Mover must first be recognized	Requires second
Main motion, limit debate, refer, postpone definitely, fix time of next meeting.	No	Yes	Yes

Amendment to the Amendment

Member:—"Mr. Chairman," (Pause for recognition) "I move that we amend the amendment by (adding, striking out, inserting, substituting) the word ———."

Chairman:—"It is moved and seconded that we amend the amendment by (state the amendment to the amendment), so that the amendment, if amended, will read that we (state the amendment as it would be changed by the amendment to the amendment). Is there any discussion on the amendment to the amendment?"

Put to VOTE (see other side at bottom of page).

Rules

1. Takes precedence of only the motion to which it applies.
2. May be amended (by "an amendment to an amendment").
3. May be divided (if incoherent) by motion to divide it, even after debate is closed.
4. Chair decides propriety of amendments, subject to appeal.
5. Chair may demand that amendments be in writing.
6. Neither yields to nor has precedence over motion to postpone indefinitely.
7. An amendment to an amendment cannot be amended. Amendments of the third degree are not permitted.
8. To table, postpone or refer an amendment to the main question is the same as tabling, postponing or referring the main question itself; consequently the motion to table, postpone or refer must be applied to the main question instead of to the amendment for the sake of clarity.

Form:—Amendments: "add, strike out, insert, strike out and insert, substitute or divide."

5	6	7	8
Debatable	Vote required	May be renewed	Motions that may apply to it
Yes	Majority	No	Amend, reconsider, limit or close debate.

Amendment to the Amendment

Put to VOTE:—"The vote is on the amendment to the amendment that we (state the amendment to the amendment). Those in favor of the amendment to the amendment say 'I.' (Pause) Those opposed say 'No'."

"I" vote:—"The 'I's' have it and the amendment to the amendment is carried. The next business is the amendment as amended which reads that we (state the amendment as amended). Is there any discussion on the amendment as amended?" (Go to Put to VOTE phrase above, opposite page.)

"No" vote:—"The 'Noes' have it and the amendment to the amendment is lost. Is there any further discussion on the original amendment?" (Go to Put to VOTE phrase above, opposite page.)

Member:—"Mr. Chairman," (Pause for recognition) "I move that we refer this question (or resolution) to (state the committee or person to which it is being referred)."

Chairman:—"It is moved and seconded that we refer this pending motion (or motions) to (state the committee or person to which it is being referred). Is there any discussion on the motion to refer?"

Put to VOTE:—"The vote is on the motion to refer the pending motion (or motions) to (state the committee or person to which it is being referred). Those in favor of the motion to refer say 'I' (Pause) Those opposed say 'No'."

"I" vote:—"The 'I's' have it and the motion to refer is carried. Is there any other business?" (Consult secretary as to next business.)

"No" vote:—"The 'Noes' have it and the motion to refer is lost. Is there any further discussion on the pending question which is (state the original motion or the amendment that is immediately pending)?"

	1	2	3	4
	May apply to the following motions	May interrupt a member who has the floor	Mover must first be recognized	Requires a second
Main motion, questions of privilege		No	Yes	Yes

To Amend the Motion to Refer

Member:—"Mr. Chairman," (Pause for recognition) "I move that we amend the motion to refer by (adding the words) (state the words to be changed)."

Chairman:—"It is moved and seconded that we amend the motion to refer by (state the amendment) so that the motion to refer if amended, will read that we (state the motion to refer as it would be changed by the amendment). Is there any discussion on the amendment to the motion to refer?"

Put to VOTE:—"The vote is on the amendment to the motion to refer which reads (state the amendment to the motion to refer). Those in favor of the amendment to the motion to refer say 'I.' (Pause) Those opposed say 'No'."

"I" vote and "No" vote (see other side, at bottom of page).

Rules

1. Debatable both as to instructions to the committee and as to the advisability of commitment.

2. May be amended by changing or instructing the committee.

3. Takes precedence over amendment to main motion, and over motion to postpone indefinitely.

4. Cannot be applied to subsidiary motions.

5. If no standing committee exists, the motion to refer should include the size of the committee and the method of selecting the members.

5	6	7	8
Debatable	Vote required	May be renewed	Motions that may apply to it
Yes (See 1)	Majority	After progress	Amend, reconsider, limit or close debate.

"I" vote:—"The 'I's' have it and the amendment to the motion to refer is carried.   The next business is the motion to refer as amended which reads that we (state motion to refer as amended). Is there any discussion on the motion to refer as amended?" (Go next to **Put to VOTE** phrase above on opposite page.)

"No" vote:—"The 'Noes' have it and the amendment to the motion to refer is lost.   Is there any discussion on the original motion to refer?" (Go next to **Put to VOTE** phrase above on opposite page.)

Member:—"Mr. Chairman" (Pause for recognition) "I move that we postpone consideration of this motion till the next meeting." (Or till the January meeting, etc.)

Chairman:—"It is moved and seconded that we postpone consideration of this motion till (state time to watch postponed). Is there any discussion as to the advisability of postponement?"

Put to VOTE:—"The vote is on the motion to postpone consideration of the pending motion (or motions) till (state time to which postponed). Those in favor of the motion to postpone definitely say 'I'. (Pause) Those opposed say 'No'."

"I" vote:—"The 'I's' have it and the motion to postpone definitely is carried. Is there any other business?" (Consult secretary as to next business.)

"No" vote:—"The 'Noes' have it and the motion to postpone definitely is lost. Is there any further discussion on the (original motion or the amendment, or whatever is immediately pending)."

1	2	3	4
May apply to the following motions.	May interrupt a member who has the floor	Mover must first be recognized	Requires a second
Main motion, questions of privilege reconsider	No	Yes	Yes

To Amend Motion to Postpone Definitely

Member:—"Mr. Chairman" (Pause for recognition) "I move that we amend the motion to postpone definitely by (state the words to be changed)."

Chairman:—"It is moved and seconded that we amend the motion to postpone definitely by (state the amendment) so that the motion to postpone definitely, if amended, will read that we (state the motion to postpone definitely as it would be changed by the amendment). Is there any discussion on the amendment to the motion to postpone definitely?"

Put to VOTE:—"The vote is on the amendment to the motion to postpone definitely which reads (state the amendment). Those in favor of the amendment to the motion to postpone definitely say 'I.' (Pause) Those opposed say 'No'."

"I" vote and "No" vote (see other side, at bottom of page).

Rules

1. Applies only to the main motion.

2. Takes precedence of motion to refer, amend, or postpone indefinitely.

3. May be amended, but only by altering the time.

4. If the intent is to create a special order for the time fixed, this motion requires a two-thirds vote.

5. The motion postponed becomes a general order for the day named and cannot be taken up sooner except by two-thirds vote, unless the motion to reconsider is still in order.

6. Debatable **only** as to the propriety of postponement.

5	6	7	8
Debatable	Vote required	May be renewed	Motions that may apply to it
Yes (See 6)	Majority (See 4)	After progress	Amend, reconsider, limit or close debate.

To Amend Motion to Postpone Definitely

"I" vote:—"The 'I's' have it and the amendment to the motion to postpone definitely is carried. The next business is the motion to postpone definitely as amended, which reads that we (state motion to postpone definitely as amended) **Is there any discussion as to the advisability of postponement?**" (Go next to **Put to VOTE** phrase above on opposite page.)

"No" vote:—"The 'Noes' have it and the amendment to the motion to postpone definitely is lost. The next business is the original motion to postpone consideration till (state the time). **Is there any discussion as to the advisability of postponement?**" (Go next to **Put to VOTE** phrase above on opposite page.)

Member:—"Mr. Chairman," (Pause for recognition) "I move that we close debate and vote immediately on the pending question." (Note:—If there are several motions pending a member may "move to close debate and vote immediately on all pending questions.)"

Chairman:—"It is moved and seconded that we close debate and vote immediately on the pending question. Those in favor of closing debate say 'I.' (Pause) Those opposed say 'No'."

"I" vote:—"The 'I's have it by a two-thirds vote and the motion to close debate is carried. The next business is the vote on the (original motion or amendment or whatever it is), which reads that we (read the immediately pending motion). Those in favor of the (original motion, amendment, or whatever it is) say 'I.' Those opposed say 'No'."

"No" vote:—"The 'Noes' have it by more than a one-third vote and the motion to close debate is lost. Is there any further discussion on the (original motion, amendment or whatever is immediately pending)?"

1	2	3	4
May apply to the following motions	May interrupt a member who has the floor	Mover must first be recognized	Requires a second.
Any debatable motion	No	Yes	Yes

To Limit Debate

Member:—"Mr. Chairman," (Pause for recognition) "I move that debate be limited (to twenty minutes or to five minutes for each speaker or to three speakers on each side) or (that debate close at ten o'clock)."

Chairman:—"It is moved and seconded that debate be limited to (twenty minutes). Those in favor say 'I.' (Pause) Those opposed say 'No'."

"I" vote:—"The 'I's' have it by a two-thirds vote and the motion to limit debate to (twenty minutes) is carried. Discussion is now on the (original motion, amendment or etc.)."

"No" vote:—"The 'Noes' have it by more than a one-third vote and the motion to limit debate is lost. Is there any discussion on the (original motion, amendment or etc.)?"

Rules

("I move the Previous Question" is the old, brief way of moving to close debate.)

1. Takes precedence of all debatable questions and all subsidiary motions except "to lay on the table".

2. Requires a two-thirds vote.

3. Its effect is confined to the immediately pending motion be it subsidiary motion, amendment, or main motion unless it specifically indicates otherwise, as, "close debate on all pending questions, or all subsidiary motions, or all motions except the main question."

4. When ordered, no additional subsidiary motion may be introduced except "to lay on the table."

5. Cannot be debated nor amended.

6. Cannot have any subsidiary motion applied to it, nor to the main question while it is pending except the motion to lay on the table.

5	6	7	8
Debatable	Vote required	May be renewed	Motions that may apply to it
No	2/3 majority	After progress	Reconsider

To Limit Debate

1. Rules same as motion to close debate, except as to amendment.
2. May be amended.
3. Does not cut off other subsidiary motions.
4. Is debatable if made as a main motion.

"Question!" "Question!"

When members of the assembly call out informally, "Question! Question!" it means only that they as individuals are ready to vote on the pending question or motion. It is their informal answer to the chairman's query, "Are your ready for the question?" This informal "call for the question" by members of the assembly must be clearly differentiated from the formal motion "to close debate and vote immediately on the pending question," or, (what is exactly the same thing) the formal "I move the Previous Question."

Member:—"Mr. Chairman," (Pause for recognition) "I move that we lay the main motion on the table."

Chairman:—"It is moved and seconded that we table the motion (state the motion). Those in favor of the motion to table say 'I.' (Pause) Those opposed say 'No'."

"I" vote:—"The 'I's' have it and the motion (state the motion) is tabled. Is there any other business?"

"No" vote:—"The 'Noes' have it and the motion to table is lost. Is there any further discussion on the motion (state the motion immediately pending)?"

1	2	3	4
May apply to the following motions	May interrupt a member who has the floor	Mover must first be recognized	Requires a second
Main question, appeals, questions of privilege, reconsideration	No	Yes	Yes

To Take From The Table

Member:—"Mr. Chairman," (Pause for recognition) "I move that we take from the table the motion to (state the motion that was **tabled**).

Chairman:—"It is moved and seconded that we take from the table the motion to (state motion that was tabled). Those in favor of taking this motion from the table say 'I.' (Pause) Those opposed say 'No'."

"I" vote:—"The 'I's' have it and the motion to take from the table is carried. You now have before you the motion to (state motion taken from the table). Is there any discussion on this motion?" (Go to page 18, left, **Put to VOTE** phrase.)

"No" vote:—"The 'Noes' have it and the motion to take from the table is lost. Is there any other business?"

1	2	3	4
May apply to the following motions	May interrupt a member who has the floor	Mover must first be recognized	Requires a second.
Only to motion that was "tabled"	No	Yes	Yes

Rules

1. Takes precedence of all other subsidiary motions.

2. May be applied to main motion, to appeals, to reconsideration, and to privileged motions that arise under questions of privilege.

3. Is in order when motion to close debate is pending or has been carried.

4. Cannot be debated or amended.

5. Not in order immediately after assembly has voted down objection to consideration.—(Has voted to consider the main motion.) (See page 11-8.)

6. Cannot have any subsidiary motion applied to it.

7. Cannot apply to any subsidiary motion.

5	6	7	8
Debatable	Vote required	May be renewed	Motions that may apply to it
No	Majority	After progress	None

To Take From The Table

Rules

1. Has status of a "special" main motion.
2. Precedence is same as any main motion.
3. May be moved same day motion was tabled.
4. Cannot be moved when any other motion is before the assembly.
5. Is not debatable. (But main motion will be debatable if taken from the table.)
6. No subsidiary motion may be applied to it. (But any subsidiary motion may be applied to the main motion if taken from the table.)

5	6	7	8
Debatable	Vote required	May be renewed	Motions that may apply to it
No	Majority	After progress	None

When seven persons desire recognition in rapid succession to make different motions the thing to do is to ignore some of them until some of the motions already before the assembly are decided by vote. The chairman has other responsibilities besides recognizing persons who desire to exhibit their technical knowledge of parliamentary procedure, and one of these other responsibilities is to keep things as simple as possible for the assembly.

However, these seven motions could be moved in this sequence and in such rapid succession that all seven would be pending at one time in strict conformity to the rules of order, but it would be nothing but a "stunt"; it would not serve any useful purpose except to illustrate the order of precedence of these seven motions and demonstrate the high privilege of the motion to adjourn in that it must be voted on at once even though these other six motions are all pending before the assembly.

Note:—If the assembly voted "No" on each of these motions in turn, then each would have to be voted upon, but in reverse order. That is, the vote would be first on the motion to adjourn. As stated above the point of order would have been decided by the chair as soon as it was raised; consequently, no vote would be required on the point of order, or on any point of information. The second vote would be on the motion to table, the third vote would be on the motion to close debate and the fourth vote would be on the motion to postpone till the next meeting. However, if the motion to close debate was defeated by a negative vote, then the chairman would be compelled to announce "The noes have it by more than a one-third vote and the motion to close debate is lost. Is there any discussion on the motion to postpone consideration till the next meeting?" Had this motion to postpone till the next meeting been voted down, the next business would have been discussion on the motion to refer. Had this motion to refer been voted down the next business would have been discussion on the amendment. Had the amendment been voted down, the next business would have been discussion on the main motion. And during discussion on the main motion any member could have moved another amendment.

Clever opponents can delay a final vote on the main motion as long as they please by clever debate and clever amendments unless the supporters of the main motion have a two-thirds vote and therefore can pass the motion "to close debate and vote immediately on all pending questions."

Of course, a majority vote in favor of the motion to adjourn would close the meeting at once. And a majority vote in favor of either the motion to lay on the table, the motion to postpone till the next meeting, the motion to refer or the motion to postpone indefinitely would immediately dispose of the main motion for the present together with all the motions pending that applied to the main motion, such as the amendment.

APPENDAGE MOTIONS (pages 16 and 19)

An amendment is a subsidiary motion, but it is a special form of subsidiary motion that may be called Appendage. An appendage motion is one that takes its rank from the motion to which it applies. Thus an amendment to the main motion takes precedence over the main motion but yields to all other motions. The amendment on page 16 is the "amendment to the main motion."

However, amendments may be made to the motion to refer, to the motion to postpone to a certain day and to the motion to limit debate. Obviously these motions could not be amended before they are voted on unless the motion to amend them took precedence over them. Therefore, the motion "to amend the main motion" does not have precedence over the motion to refer. But the motion "to amend the motion to refer" does take precedence over the motion to refer, but not over the motion to postpone to a certain day. Similarly the motion "to amend the motion to postpone to a certain day" must take precedence over the motion "to postpone to a certain day" but not over the "motion to close debate."

Thus the motion to amend is a special form of subsidiary motion called "appendage motion" because it has no absolute rank, but instead takes its rank from the motion to which it applies.

The motion to reconsider is the other appendage motion. Because it is an appendage motion and also has special rules as to who can move it and as to when it may be moved, the motion to reconsider is the most complicated of all motions. This motion is not classified at all in most manuals because it applies to the "vote" on the motion and not to the motion itself. However, it is as pure an example of the appendage principle as is the motion to amend in that it takes its precedence (and in fact most other features of its status) from the motion to which it applies.

Purpose, Precedence, and Strategic Use of Motions.

In the Appendix at the back of the manual is a brief explanation of the purpose, precedence, and strategic use of the more important motions.

HOW TO USE MANUAL
The Eight Phases of Each Motion

Each motion has eight different phases or aspects that are indicated by the following eight questions.

1. May this motion apply to other motions?
2. May the mover of this motion interrupt another member who is speaking?
3. Must a member be recognized by the chair before he can make this motion?
4. Must this motion be seconded before it is officially before the assembly?
5. Is this motion debatable?
6. What vote is required for its adoption?
7. May this motion be renewed after it has been voted down?
8. What other motions may apply to this motion?

Any good text on parliamentary procedure will answer all eight of these questions on each motion. But it would take the ordinary person many minutes, perhaps an hour, to find the answer to these eight questions on any one motion in these standard texts.

In this manual the answer to any one of these eight questions on any motion may be found in just two seconds by turning to this motion in the "finder index" at the center of the book and looking at the chart in the middle of that page. Thus under the main motion, page 18, will be found this chart.

1	2	3	4
May apply to the following Motions	May interrupt a member who has the floor	Mover must first be recognized	Requires a second
No other motion	No	Yes	Yes

5	6	7	8
Debatable	Vote required	May be renewed	Motions that may apply to it
Yes	Majority	Not at same session	All

Here are the correct answers to these eight questions and these answers will be found in exactly this order under each motion. Thus item number 5 is "Debatable" and the answer is "yes" for a main motion. It should not take very long to learn where to look on this chart for the answer to each question. And once this sequence is learned, the answer to any one of the eight questions about any one of the eight motions may be found in less than two seconds.

For instance, someone may ask, "Is the motion to refer debatable?" Open the manual to the center where the motions are listed in a finder-index, place your thumb on the page that is headed "To Refer," throw the manual open at that page (page 15), look at item 5 in the chart (first item on right hand page) and read:

	5	
	Debatable	
	Yes	

Thus the information is available in a second, it is in plain English, not in a code, and it is correct because these rules are in accordance with the Congressional Manual and other standard texts on Rules of Order (parliamentary procedure).

In brief, this manual eliminates the necessity for memorizing the many, many rules of parliamentary procedure, and permits the chairman to concentrate on maintaining order in the assembly and on making it clear to the assembly as to what is before them for consideration and vote. This manual also enables a member to check up on these rules in a second, before he makes a motion, to be sure that his motion is in order and that he is moving it in the proper manner.

Proper Phraseology

In addition to giving the rules of procedure for each motion, this manual also provides the proper form for stating each motion when a member is moving it, and the proper phrases for the chairman to use when restating the motion to the assembly, when putting it to a vote and when stating the result of an "I" vote or a "No" vote.

The phrase to be used by a member in making the motion is in ordinary type at the top of the left hand page following the word "Member." The phrases for the chairman to use are in bold-faced type on the left hand page following the word "Chairman."

Parliamentary Phrases for a Chairman

The amateur chairman will do well to read these phrases directly from the manual in handling any motion because these phrases are correct, they are complete, and they lead the chairman safely and quickly through the discussion, the vote, the result of the vote, and thence to what is next to come before the assembly.

A proud chairman should not disdain to use these mechanical aids because the Speaker of the United States House of Representatives has two parliamentary assistants to aid him in addition to the regular clerk of the House. The clerk on the speaker's left is called the time-keeper, and he keeps a check on time allotted to each member who speaks, but he helps in other ways, such as by identifying quickly congressmen who rise to speak. The clerk on the speaker's right is called the parliamentarian and it is his duty to check up on all fine points of procedure that arise, but he likewise helps to identify new members of Congress when they arise to speak.

Being a good chairman is a large undertaking and no chairman should neglect to use all the help he can find, because correctness is of first importance with a chairman, and correctness is a matter of fact not a matter of conceit.

"Aye" Versus "I" for "Yes"

Common usage today is to spell the adverb meaning yes—"a-y-e" and pronounce it the same as the pronoun "I." Unfortunately, the adverb meaning forever is spelled the same way but pronounced differently—is spelled "a-y-e" but pronounced "A." Because of these two distinct pronunciations for the same combination of letters there is constant confusion as to whether the vote "Aye" should be pronounced "I" or "A." To avoid this confusion the word "Aye" is not used in this manual at all. In its place will be found the pronoun "I" which may be taken either as a phonetic spelling for the adverb "Aye" meaning yes, or as an abbreviated form of "I vote for it." Inasmuch as Shakespeare always used the letter "I" for the adverb meaning yes, there is excellent literary authority for this usage in addition to its practical utility. (See original ("Globe") edition of Shakespeare.)

APPENDIX

Purpose and Precedence of Motions

MAIN QUESTION (or Motion)

The main question or motion is the main idea before the group, such as a motion to have a dance or a motion to raise the dues. Obviously, it would lead to confusion to have members discussing two different ideas at the same time; hence the rule that only one main motion can be before the assembly at any one time, and the correlative rule that a main motion can not be introduced when any other motion is before the group.

AMENDMENTS

Amendments are for the purpose of changing a motion before that motion comes up for a final vote. Amendments may be quite difficult for a chairman to handle because they vary all the way from short, simple amendments to long, complicated ones; from clever, time-wasting amendments to ridiculous but well-meaning ones. Which to permit and which to declare out of order must be decided by the Chair promptly upon the basis of plain common sense. It is frequently quite difficult for the chairman to differentiate between the clever amendment with evil intent that frequently should be declared out of order, and the awkward but well-meaning amendment that should be permitted even though the secretary may have to re-word it in order that it may make sense. It is a part of the chairman's business to help the dumb or ignorant member formulate the amendment he has in mind but can not state in proper parliamentary form. On the other hand, it is equally important that the chairman prevent the smart-Aleck member from wasting the time of the assembly with well-formulated but purely obstructionist motions. Sound judgment and a forceful personality are both requisites of a first class chairman.

Another difficulty connected with amendments is the matter of their precedence, because an amendment is necessarily an "appendage" to another motion; consequently, it must always have precedence over the motion to which it applies. In the manual index it is given low precedence, but this is only for amendments to the main motion, and the main motion has the lowest precedence of all the motions. Obviously, an amendment to the motion to refer must have precedence over the motion to refer. Likewise, an amendment to the motion to limit debate must have precedence over the motion to limit debate. Finally, if no time has been fixed for the next meeting and some one moves that the "time for the next meeting be Friday evening," then an amendment to this motion "fixing the time for the next meeting" must of necessity have precedence over **all other motions**. This is so because the motion "to fix the time for the next meeting" (when no such time has yet been fixed) takes precedence over all other motions, and an amendment to it must of necessity have precedence over it. Hence the rule that an amendment takes precedence over the motion to which it applies, so that its absolute precedence is simply that of the motion to which it applies. In short, it is an appendage motion.

MOTION TO RECONSIDER

The motion to reconsider is another "appendage" motion that takes its precedence from the motion to which it applies. Thus the motion to **"reconsider the vote on the motion to close debate"** must be acted on at once because you can not proceed with the business before the assembly until you have finally settled the question as to whether you are or are not going to close debate. Obviously, the motion to reconsider suspends action on the motion to which it applies until the motion to reconsider has been acted on. For this reason the motion to reconsider must be acted on at once if it applies to the motion to close debate. But it need not be acted on at once if it applies to the main motion or to a subsidiary motion that does not require immediate action.

An especially difficult feature of the motion to reconsider is that it has one precedence for entry (for moving it) and another precedence for actual consideration and vote. The reason for this difference in the precedence of two different phases of the same motion is that the motion to reconsider is in order **only for a brief period,** usually not more than one day after the vote on the motion to which it applies. Consequently, the motion to reconsider must be moved when it is still in order. If certain other business is before the assembly when you decide that you would like to move reconsideration on a motion that was voted on yesterday, this other business before the assembly may not be disposed of until after the time for moving reconsideration of yesterday's motion has expired. It is in view of this frequent possibility that a member is permitted to "interrupt other business," may even "interrupt a member who has the floor and is speaking" in order to move reconsideration on a motion that has already been voted on. However, when the motion to reconsider has been moved and therefore entered on the minutes, it need not be acted on at once, because it automatically suspends action on the motion to which it applies.

When a pending question is interrupted by a member who desires to move reconsideration on a former main motion, this pending question is resumed immediately after the interruption and disposed of. Then, when there is no other business before the assembly, this motion to reconsider, previously moved, should be taken up and disposed of. For consideration and vote the motion to reconsider has only the precedence of the motion to which it applies; consequently, if it applies to a main motion it can only be taken up for consideration and vote when there is no other business before the assembly. But (for the reasons given above) the motion to reconsider the vote on a former main motion has high privilege for entry (that is, to be moved).

Reconsideration of an affirmative vote on a subsidiary motion has much the same status as reconsideration of a main motion, because such an affirmative vote disposes of the main motion temporarily at least, and, therefore, this reconsideration is much the same as reconsideration of the vote on the main motion itself. Thus reconsideration of an affirmative vote on the motion to refer brings both the motion to refer and the main motion back before the assembly for consideration. However, reconsideration of an affirmative vote on the motion to close debate must be moved immediately after the vote on the motion to close debate because obviously there would be no point to moving reconsideration on the motion to close debate after the main motion had been disposed of. (The motion to close debate provides for an immediate vote on the pending question.)

A negative vote on a subsidiary, incidental, or privileged motion can not be reconsidered except immediately after the vote is taken for the obvious reason that "after progress" these subsidiary, incidental, and privileged motions may, as a rule, be "renewed." Thus when the motion to close debate has been voted down and then debate has proceeded for some time, the way to close debate is not by moving reconsideration of the former vote on the motion to close debate. On the contrary, the quickest and least confusing way is simply to move again that "debate be closed," since this motion may be "renewed" after progress.

CLINCHING THE MOTION (by Reconsideration)

A common parliamentary trick called "clinching the motion" involves the use of the motion to reconsider, but in this case the motion to reconsider is moved, not by one who has suddenly changed his mind about the motion just voted on, but by one who voted with the majority and wants to "clinch" this majority victory before some member of the majority does change his mind. Immediately after the majority passes or defeats a motion the majority leader moves that this vote be reconsidered. Then the majority votes down the motion to reconsider so that if, later, some members of the majority do change their minds about the main motion that was voted on, they can not then move reconsideration because the rule is that "No motion may be twice reconsidered." Also, this method is used when a motion is passed by the assembly which should go into effect at once. Since the law can not be put into effect so long as the motion to reconsider may be moved, the way to speed its being put into effect is for the majority to move reconsideration immediately and then vote down reconsideration.

The minority frequently use the motion to reconsider as a means of delaying final action on a motion, but the majority can forestall this use of the motion by moving it themselves and then immediately voting it down. "What is sauce for the goose is sauce for the gander." (The motion to reconsider may be moved only by those who voted with the prevailing side, but this difficulty is easily solved by the minority by the simple device of having two members of the minority vote with the majority in order thus to qualify themselves to move and second the motion to reconsider.)

ADJOURNMENT

The motion to adjourn is one of the most common motions and one of the most highly privileged, provided the time for the next meeting is already determined, as it usually is in most organizations. When privileged, the motion to adjourn can be moved at almost any time and must be voted on at once because it is not debatable when privileged. However, the motion to adjourn is not privileged when no time has been fixed for the next meeting, because adjournment without time being fixed for the next meeting simply breaks up the organization, dissolves the assembly. When not privileged, the motion to adjourn can be moved only when there is no other business before the assembly, and in that case it is debatable. Also, in such a case, the motion to adjourn yields to the motion "to fix the time for the next meeting," for obvious reasons.

QUESTIONS OF PRIVILEGE

A common point for confusion is the difference between a question of privilege and a privileged question or motion. A question of privilege has to do with the rights and comforts of the assembly as a whole, or the rights and comfort of any member. As such, these rights are given immediate consideration regardless of what else is before the assembly. Thus if the room becomes too hot, a member may even interrupt a speaker in order to ask the chairman to provide adequate ventilation. When a motion is before the assembly and certain points of a confidential nature are brought up, any member may "rise to a question of privilege," and when the chairman says, "State your question of privilege," the member may say, "As a question of privilege I move that the visitors be asked to leave the room while this confidential matter is being discussed." If the chairman decides that conditions warrant granting this privilege he says, "As a question of privilege it is moved and seconded that the visitors be asked to leave the room while this confidential matter is being discussed. Is there any discussion on this privileged motion?"

The question of whether a member may demand better ventilation or may ask to be excused from the remainder of the meeting are questions of privilege. It is also a question of privilege when a member asks permission to interrupt a speaker and move that the room be cleared of visitors, or that the assembly go immediately to another room where it is warmer or where the light is better. Thus it is a question of privilege when another member asks permission to do something or to have something done which he could not do or could not have done under the ordinary rules of procedure. And the Chair decides immediately the point as to whether or not this **special** privilege is to be granted. Such a grant of privilege does not require any vote unless some member appeals from the decision of the Chair. (See Appeals, page 6.)

If, however, this question of privilege involves the right to make a motion and this privilege is granted by the Chair, then the motion made under this grant of special privilege becomes a **privileged motion** that must be disposed of by vote before the assembly can proceed with the business that was before it when this question of privilege was raised.

PRIVILEGED MOTIONS

A privileged motion is a motion of such a nature that it must be disposed of immediately, regardless of the other business that may be pending. The privileged motions are:—to fix the time for the next meeting (when no such time has been fixed); to adjourn (when privileged). (See above under Adjournment); to call for **orders of the day** (when there are such orders); and motions made under the grant of privilege by the chair to a member who has "risen to a question of privilege."

RISING TO A POINT OF ORDER

Whenever a member believes that the Chair has made a mistake or a wrong decision, the member may rise to a point of order by saying as he rises (and without waiting to be recognized by the Chair), "Mr. Chairman, I rise to a point of order." This may even interrupt another member who has the floor and is speaking. The chairman should then say, "State your point of order." When the member states the point of order, the chairman decides, "Your point is **not** well taken," and then proceeds with whatever business is before the assembly, or he decides, "Your point **is** well taken," and then proceeds with whatever business is in order under the **reversed** ruling.

APPEALS

If any member is dissatisfied with any decision made by the Chair, he may appeal from this decision of the Chair **to the assembly** by rising and saying (without waiting to be recognized), "I appeal from the decision of the Chair." An appeal requires a second. One disgruntled member is not enough to warrant a vote of the assembly on a decision of the Chair. When there is such an appeal, **the chairman states the reasons for his decision** (if he desires to give reasons), and then calls for a vote by saying, "Those in favor of sustaining the decision of the Chair say 'I'. Those opposed to sustaining the decision of the Chair say 'No'." (See under motion to Appeal, page 6.)

DILATORY APPEALS

However, the Chair usually refuses to permit an appeal when the purpose of the appeal is obviously to delay action or to annoy the chairman. Here, as in every other act, the chairman must maintain his position of fairness and impartiality. It seldom pays to "steam roll" the minority even though the chairman knows that he has the undivided support of the majority. Common sense is the essence of parliamentary rules; fairplay is their guiding principle; reasonable discussion followed by prompt action is what they are devised to achieve.

OBJECTION TO CONSIDERATION

Objection to consideration is a motion that is not often used, but it is invaluable when needed. Its purpose is to prevent any discussion on a motion when either the motion or the discussion on it is quite objectionable to a large majority of the group. Since its purpose is to eliminate undesirable motions, it applies only to the main motion and to questions of privilege, because these are the only two methods of bringing unexpected subjects before the assembly. Also, since its further purpose is to prevent any discussion on this undesirable motion, a member may interrupt a speaker in order to move "objection to consideration." And since only one member may know of the evil involved in the undesirable motion, the motion "objection to consideration" does not require a second. However, two-thirds of the members must be against consideration in order thus to eliminate a motion without any discussion whatsoever. (For the phrasing of this difficult question and putting it to a vote see page 11, under "Objection to Consideration.") One little point in this connection that may easily be overlooked in the manual is that the motion to lay on the table is out of order immediately after "objection to consideration" has been defeated. That is to say, when one more than one-third of the assembly vote in favor of "considering the motion" (It takes a two-thirds vote in the negative to prevent consideration), it is not then permissible for a bare majority of 51 per cent to lay aside the motion objected to, without any discussion, by means of the motion to lay on the table which is not debatable and requires only a majority vote. However, after there has been several minutes of discussion on the undesirable motion, the motion to lay on the table is in order and may be applied. Stated briefly, if objection to consideration is moved against a certain motion and one more than one-third of the assembly vote in favor of considering the motion, then a few minutes of discussion must be permitted on the undesirable motion before it is disposed of.

The question may well be asked, "Why not move to lay on the

table the undesirable motion in the first place?", since a bare majority can pass the motion to lay on the table and this subsidiary motion is undebatable. There are two reasons why the motion to lay on the table does not serve as well as the motion "objection to consideration" in disposing of very bad motions. The first reason is that a motion "laid on the table" may be "taken from the table" by a simple majority vote at any time after it has been "laid on the table." Consequently, a motion that is "tabled" may be only temporarily disposed of, whereas a motion "thrown out" by "objection to consideration" can not be brought before the assembly again at that session. The second reason is that the motion to "table" can not be moved when another member has the floor. Consequently, if some crank makes a motion, gets it seconded, and then starts to make a crazy or nasty speech on it, he can not be interrupted by the motion to "table", because the motion to "table" may not be moved when another member has the floor. But "objection to consideration" may be moved when another member has the floor; consequently, it may be used to stop a speaker right in the midst of his speech, provided two-thirds of the assembly are in favor of preventing "consideration of the motion." To repeat, objection to consideration is a motion that is not often used, but it is invaluable when needed.

PARLIAMENTARY STRATEGY

Strategic Use of the Motion to Postpone Indefinitely

The motion to postpone indefinitely is not a useful motion from the standpoint of its direct effect, because it is just as easy to vote down the main motion as it is to pass the motion to postpone indefinitely, since both are debatable and both have the lowest possible precedence. The real value of the motion to postpone indefinitely is strategic. It is the motion by which the opposition to a motion can ascertain the number of members for and against the main motion without the risk of having the main motion adopted.

If, at a national luncheon club convention, someone moves that the dues be increased ten dollars per member, those opposed to this increase in dues should move at once to postpone consideration of this motion indefinitely. Then they should present all their general arguments against the increase. When the vote is finally taken on the motion to postpone indefinitely, the opposition to the increase in dues are in the position of advantage. If the motion to postpone indefinitely is carried, the motion to increase the dues ten dollars is "thrown out" and can not be brought up again at that convention. On the other hand, if the motion to postpone indefinitely is defeated, the opponents of the raise in dues still have the advantage of having learned how large a majority are in favor of the increase, thus enabling them to determine just how many members now in favor of the increase must be won over to the opposition in order to defeat the main motion when it comes up for final vote.

In short, the motion to postpone indefinitely is the strategic motion used by the opposition to reveal the strength of the advocates of the main motion without the risk of having the main motion adopted. Having secured this information, the leaders of the opposition are better able to plan their political campaign against the final passage of the main motion.

(Note:—For detailed instructions as to the duties of officers and committees, as to the conduct of committee meetings (especially committee of the whole) and as to the formulation and acceptance of committee reports, consult the larger treatises on parliamentary or legislative procedure.)

Lesson IX

DIVISION OF VOTE AND POINTS OF ORDER

There are several little items of procedure that are not exactly motions, and yet they play an important part in parliamentary affairs. The first of these is "calling for a division of vote." Any member of an assembly has the right to "demand" a vote that can be counted if he is dissatisfied with the chairman's decision on a vote by sound, that is, "I" and "No" vote. Thus when the chairman thinks that the "I's" have it and the motion is carried, any member of the assembly may, without rising, call out, "Mr. Chairman, I call for a division of vote." Or he may simply call out, "Division." This one demand requires the chairman to have a show of hands or a rising vote that may be counted. (See page 10 in manual.)

When a "division" has been called for and the vote is close the chairman should count the votes and then announce the count so that the assembly will not be in doubt as to just which side won.

A vote by ballot has the advantage that it can be counted without revealing how each person voted. Voting by ballot is desirable when there is considerable feeling on a question or when officers are being nominated or elected. However, voting by ballot cannot be demanded by one member. To order voting by ballot requires a regular motion, such as, "Mr. Chairman, I move that this vote be by ballot." This motion must be seconded and carried by a majority vote. In ordinary class drills in procedure voting by ballot should be prohibited simply because it takes too much time. (See page 10 in manual.)

A second item of procedure that is much used is "rising to a point of order." Like calling for a division of vote, "rising to a point of order" may occur at any time, even when another person is speaking. The purpose of "rising to a point of order" is to call the chairman's attention to the fact that he has made a mistake or that some member of the assembly has made a mistake. Thus if one main motion is before the assembly and someone moves a second main motion, the chairman should declare the second main motion "out of order." But if the chairman makes the mistake of thinking this second motion is "in order," some member of the assembly should arise and say, (without waiting to be recognized by the chair), "Mr. Chairman, I rise to a point of order." The chairman should reply, "State your point of order." The member who rose should then say, "This last motion is out of order because there is already one main motion before the assembly." If the chairman sees his mistake he should say, "Your point is well taken. This last motion is out of order." If the chairman does not see that he has made a mistake he should say, "Your point is *not* well taken. This last motion is in order." (See page 5 in manual.)

A third privilege of members that is somewhat similar to a point of order is "rising for information." When a member desires to ask a question he rises and says, without waiting to be recognized, "Mr. Chairman, I rise for information." The chairman replies, "State your question." The member then states his question as, "What time does this meeting close?" or "When do we meet tomorrow?" or "Is an amendment in order at this time?" (See bottom of page 5 in manual.)

The purpose of this practice is to demonstrate the use of "points of order," "rising for information," and "calling for a division of vote." By having this practice in the form of a majority-minority contest it will become evident that the minority members have more use for these new points of procedure than the majority members.

Chairman:—"THE MEETING WILL COME TO ORDER. BUSINESS IS NOW IN ORDER."

Majority Leader:—"MR. CHAIRMAN."

Chairman:—"MR. MAJORITY LEADER."

Majority Leader:—"I MOVE THAT WE FIRE OUR INSTRUCTOR."

Minority Leader:—"MR. CHAIRMAN, I RISE TO A POINT OF ORDER."

Chairman:—"STATE YOUR POINT OF ORDER."

Minority Leader:—"THE HIRING AND FIRING OF TEACHERS IS THE BUSINESS OF THE SUPERINTENDENT AND NOT THE BUSINESS OF THIS CLASS. THEREFORE, THIS MOTION TO FIRE THE INSTRUCTOR IS OUT OF ORDER BECAUSE IT IS BEYOND OUR AUTHORITY."

Chairman:—"YOUR POINT IS WELL TAKEN. THE MOTION IS OUT OF ORDER. IS THERE ANY OTHER BUSINESS?"

Majority Leader:—"MR. CHAIRMAN, I MOVE THAT WE HAVE A ————." *(Chairman interrupts.)*

Chairman:—"YOU ARE OUT OF ORDER. YOU HAVE NOT BEEN RECOGNIZED BY THE CHAIR."

Majority Leader:—"MR. CHAIRMAN."

Chairman:—"MR. MAJORITY LEADER."

Majority Leader:—"I MOVE THAT WE HAVE PARLIA-MENTARY DRILL EVERY DAY."

Majority Leader's Assistant calls out, "I SECOND THE MO-TION."

Chairman:—"IT IS MOVED AND SECONDED THAT WE HAVE PARLIAMENTARY DRILL EVERY DAY. IS THERE ANY DISCUSSION?"

Minority Leader:—"MR. CHAIRMAN."

Chairman:—"MR. MINORITY LEADER."

Minority Leader:—"I MOVE THAT WE REFER THIS MAT-TER TO THE EXECUTIVE COMMITTEE."

Minority Leader's Assistant calls out, "I SECOND THE MO-TION."

Chairman:—"IT IS MOVED AND SECONDED THAT WE REFER THIS MATTER TO THE EXECUTIVE COM-MITTEE. IS THERE ANY DISCUSSION ON THE MO-TION TO REFER?"

Minority Leader:—"MR. CHAIRMAN."

Chairman:—"MR. MINORITY LEADER."

Minority Leader:—"I MOVE THAT WE AMEND THE ORIGINAL MOTION BY INSERTING THE WORD 'OTHER' BEFORE THE WORD 'DAY'."

Chairman:—"IS THERE A SECOND?"

Majority Leader:—"MR. CHAIRMAN, I RISE TO A POINT OF ORDER."

Chairman:—"STATE YOUR POINT OF ORDER."

Majority Leader:—"THE MOTION TO REFER DOES NOT YIELD TO THE MOTION TO AMEND. THERE-FORE THIS MOTION TO AMEND IS OUT OF ORDER."

Chairman:—"YOUR POINT IS WELL TAKEN. THE MO-TION TO AMEND IS OUT OF ORDER. IS THERE ANY FURTHER DISCUSSION ON THE MOTION TO REFER?"

Chairman:—"ARE YOU READY FOR THE QUESTION?"

Several members call out, "QUESTION!" *(See bottom of page 13 in manual.)*

Chairman:—"THE VOTE IS ON THE MOTION TO REFER TO THE EXECUTIVE COMMITTEE THE QUESTION OF HAVING PARLIAMENTARY DRILL EVERY DAY. THOSE IN FAVOR OF THE MOTION TO REFER SAY 'I'." *(Some of the assembly vote "I".)* "THOSE OPPOSED SAY 'NO'." *(Some of the assembly vote "No.")*

Majority Leader calls out, "DIVISION."

Chairman:—"A DIVISION OF VOTE HAS BEEN CALLED FOR. THOSE IN FAVOR OF THE MOTION TO REFER TO THE EXECUTIVE COMMITTEE PLEASE RAISE THEIR RIGHT HAND." *(Pause while hands are counted, minority vote "I".)* "THOSE OPPOSED PLEASE RAISE THEIR RIGHT HAND." *(Pause while hands are counted. Majority vote "No.")*

Chairman:—"THE VOTE IS 13 FOR AND 17 AGAINST. THE 'NOES' HAVE IT AND THE MOTION TO REFER IS LOST. THE NEXT BUSINESS IS THE ORIGINAL MOTION THAT WE HAVE PARLIAMENTARY DRILL EVERY DAY. IS THERE ANY DISCUSSION ON THE ORIGINAL MOTION?"

Minority Leader:—"MR. CHAIRMAN, I RISE FOR IN-FORMATION."

Chairman:—"STATE YOUR QUESTION."

Minority Leader:—"IS AN AMENDMENT IN ORDER AT THIS TIME?"

Chairman:—"IT IS."

Minority Leader:—"THEN I MOVE THAT WE AMEND THE MOTION BY INSERTING THE WORD 'OTHER' BEFORE THE WORD 'DAY'."

Minority Leader's Assistant calls, "I SECOND THE MO-TION."

Chairman:—"IT IS MOVED AND SECONDED THAT WE AMEND THE MOTION BY INSERTING THE WORD 'OTHER' BEFORE THE WORD 'DAY' SO THAT THE MOTION, IF AMENDED, WILL READ THAT WE HAVE PARLIAMENTARY DRILL EVERY *OTHER* DAY. IS THERE ANY DISCUSSION ON THE AMEND-MENT?"

Majority Leader:—"MR. CHAIRMAN, I RISE FOR IN-FORMATION."

Chairman:—"STATE YOUR QUESTION."

Majority Leader:—"HOW MUCH TIME IS THERE YET BEFORE THE BELL RINGS?"

Chairman:—"SIX MINUTES."

Majority Leader:—"THEN I MOVE THAT WE CLOSE DEBATE AND VOTE IMMEDIATELY ON *ALL PENDING QUESTIONS.*"

Majority Leader's Assistant calls out, "I SECOND THE MOTION."

Chairman:—"IT IS MOVED AND SECONDED THAT WE CLOSE DEBATE AND VOTE IMMEDIATELY ON *ALL* PENDING QUESTIONS." *(Interruption.)*

Minority Leader interrupts by rising and saying loudly, "MR. CHAIRMAN, I RISE FOR INFORMATION."

Chairman:—"STATE YOUR QUESTION."

Minority Leader:—"IS THE MOTION TO LAY ON THE TABLE IN ORDER NOW?"

Chairman:—"IT IS. THE MOTION TO CLOSE DEBATE YIELDS TO THE MOTION TO LAY ON THE TABLE."

Minority Leader:—"THEN I MOVE THAT WE LAY THE ORIGINAL MOTION AND THE AMENDMENT ON THE TABLE."

Minority Leader's Assistant calls out, "I SECOND THE MOTION."

Chairman:—"IT IS MOVED AND SECONDED THAT WE LAY THE ORIGINAL MOTION ON THE TABLE. THOSE IN FAVOR ——." *(Interruption.)*

Minority Leader interrupts again, "MR. CHAIRMAN, I RISE TO A POINT OF ORDER."

Chairman:—"STATE YOUR POINT OF ORDER."

Minority Leader:—"MY MOTION WAS TO LAY BOTH THE ORIGINAL MOTION AND THE AMENDMENT ON THE TABLE."

Chairman:—"TECHNICALLY YOU ARE CORRECT AS TO WORDING. BUT IF YOU LAY THE ORIGINAL MOTION ON THE TABLE IT TAKES THE AMENDMENT WITH IT. THEREFORE, IT MAKES NO DIFFERENCE WHETHER THE AMENDMENT IS MENTIONED OR NOT MENTIONED. THE RESULT IS EXACTLY THE SAME IN EITHER CASE. THOSE IN FAVOR

OF THE MOTION TO LAY ON THE TABLE SAY "I"." *(Some vote "I".)* "THOSE OPPOSED SAY 'NO'." *(Some vote "No".)*

Chairman:—"THE CHAIR IS IN DOUBT. THOSE IN FAVOR OF THE MOTION TO LAY ON THE TABLE PLEASE STAND UP. *(Ten stand up.)* BE SEATED. THOSE OPPOSED PLEASE STAND UP. *(Twenty stand up.)* BE SEATED."

Chairman:—"THE VOTE IS TEN FOR AND TWENTY AGAINST. THE 'NOES' HAVE IT AND THE MOTION TO LAY ON THE TABLE IS LOST. THE NEXT BUSINESS IS THE VOTE ON THE MOTION TO CLOSE DEBATE AND VOTE IMMEDIATELY ON *ALL* PENDING QUESTIONS." *(Interruption.)*

Minority Leader interrupts again:—"MR. CHAIRMAN."

Chairman:—"MR. MINORITY LEADER."

Minority Leader:—"I MOVE THAT WE ADJOURN."

Minority Leader's Assistant calls out, "I SECOND THE MOTION."

Chairman:—"IT IS MOVED AND SECONDED THAT WE ADJOURN. THOSE IN FAVOR OF ADJOURNMENT SAY 'I'." *(A few say "I".)* "THOSE OPPOSED SAY 'NO'." *(Many say "No".)*

Minority Leader:—"DIVISION."

Chairman:—"A DIVISION HAS BEEN CALLED FOR. THOSE IN FAVOR OF ADJOURNMENT PLEASE STAND UP. *(Ten stand up.)* BE SEATED. THOSE OPPOSED TO ADJOURNMENT PLEASE STAND UP. *(Twenty stand up.)* BE SEATED."

Chairman:—"THE VOTE IS TEN FOR AND TWENTY AGAINST. THE 'NOES' HAVE IT AND THE MOTION TO ADJOURN IS LOST. THE NEXT BUSINESS IS THE VOTE ON THE MOTION TO CLOSE DEBATE AND VOTE IMMEDIATELY ON ALL PENDING QUESTIONS. THOSE IN FAVOR OF THE MOTION TO CLOSE DEBATE ON ALL PENDING QUESTIONS PLEASE STAND UP. *(Twenty stand up.)* BE SEATED. THOSE OPPOSED TO THE MOTION TO CLOSE DEBATE ON ALL PENDING QUESTIONS PLEASE STAND UP. *(Ten stand up.)* BE SEATED."

Chairman:—"THE VOTE IS TWENTY FOR AND TEN AGAINST. THE 'I's' HAVE IT BY A TWO-THIRDS VOTE AND THE MOTION TO CLOSE DEBATE ON ALL PENDING QUESTIONS IS CARRIED. THE NEXT BUSINESS IS THE VOTE ON THE AMENDMENT WHICH READS THAT WE INSERT THE WORD 'OTHER' BEFORE THE WORD 'DAY'. THOSE IN FAVOR OF THE AMENDMENT—" *(Interruption.)*

A member of the assembly rises saying, "MR. CHAIRMAN, I RISE FOR INFORMATION."

Chairman:—"STATE YOUR QUESTION."

Member:—"JUST HOW WILL THIS AMENDMENT AFFECT THE ORIGINAL MOTION?"

Chairman:—"IT WILL CHANGE THE TIME FROM 'EVERY DAY' TO 'EVERY OTHER DAY'. THOSE IN FAVOR OF THE AMENDMENT SAY 'I'." *(A few vote "I".)* "THOSE OPPOSED SAY 'NO'." *(Many vote "No".)*

Chairman:—"THE 'NOES' SEEM TO HAVE IT."

Minority Leader:—"DIVISION."

Chairman:—"THOSE IN FAVOR OF THE AMENDMENT PLEASE RAISE THE RIGHT HAND. *(Twelve raise their hand.)* THOSE OPPOSED PLEASE RAISE THEIR RIGHT HAND." *(Eighteen raise their hand.)*

Chairman:—"THE VOTE IS TWELVE FOR AND EIGHTEEN AGAINST. THE 'NOES' HAVE IT AND THE AMENDMENT IS LOST. THE NEXT BUSINESS IS THE VOTE ON THE ORIGINAL MOTION WHICH READS THAT WE HAVE PARLIAMENTARY DRILL EVERY DAY. THOSE IN FAVOR OF THIS MOTION SAY 'I'." *(Many vote "I".)* "THOSE OPPOSED SAY 'NO'." *(A few vote "No".)*

Minority Leader:—"DIVISION."

Chairman:—"A DIVISION OF VOTE HAS BEEN CALLED FOR. THOSE IN FAVOR OF THE MOTION TO HAVE PARLIAMENTARY DRILL EVERY DAY PLEASE STAND UP. *(Sixteen stand up.)* BE SEATED. THOSE OPPOSED TO THIS MOTION PLEASE STAND UP. *(Fourteen stand up.)* BE SEATED."

Chairman:—"THE VOTE IS SIXTEEN FOR AND FOURTEEN AGAINST. THE 'I's' HAVE IT AND THE MOTION TO HAVE PARLIAMENTARY DRILL EVERY DAY IS CARRIED. IS THERE ANY OTHER BUSINESS?"

Majority Leader:—"MR. CHAIRMAN."

Chairman:—"MR. MAJORITY LEADER."

Majority Leader:—"I MOVE THAT WE ADJOURN."

Majority Leader's Assistant calls out, "I SECOND THE MO-TION."

Chairman:—"IT IS MOVED AND SECONDED THAT WE ADJOURN. THOSE IN FAVOR SAY 'I'." *(Many vote "I".)* "THOSE OPPOSED SAY 'NO'." *(A few vote "No".)*

Chairman:—"THE 'I's' HAVE IT AND THE MOTION TO ADJOURN IS CARRIED. YOU STAND ADJOURN-ED." *(Chairman sounds the gavel.)*

Continue as many different majority-minority con-tests as time will permit, having a different student chairman, and different floor leaders for each contest. If the majority is winning the contests too easily, re-divide the groups so that the minority will have a few more than a third of the total. This should enable the minority to win. After each contest the mis-takes of the chairman and of each group should be pointed out and corrected. Also opportunity should be given for questions. When the minority succeed in preventing a final vote on the main question for more than five minutes the minority should be de-clared the winner immediately without waiting for the vote on the pending motions.

Another way to equalize this contest is to lengthen or short-en the time limit. If the majority must get their motion passed within five minutes the minority have a good chance to win even though they have less than a one-third vote. On the other hand the dumbest and slowest majority leader ought to get the main motion passed within fifteen minutes if the majority has a two-thirds vote.

LEADERSHIP MONOPOLY

When certain members of the class become so proficient and so outspoken as to tend to monopolize the leadership in these contests, these outspoken students should be required to remain seated and write a criticism of what the majority and minority leaders do. They may also be required to criticise the chairman's conduct of the contest. These written criticisms should be hand-ed to the instructor at the end of the contests. They should be graded, and the instructor should insert written comments on their accuracy, completeness and keenness before returning them to the students who wrote them.

1.

My mover does not have to be recognized.
I do not require a second.
The chairman must grant my demand unless conditions are quite exceptional.
I am useful in securing an accurate count of the vote.
What am I?

2.

My mover need not wait to be recognized.
I do not require a second or a vote.
I am used to correct the chairman.
What am I?

3.

I am usually not debatable but I require a second.
I may be renewed after progress.
I am almost always in order.
What am I?

4.

I do not require a second.
My mover need not be recognized before I am stated.
My purpose is not to correct the chairman.
I am used to ask a question.
What am I?

Note:—"Calling for a division" and "rising to a point of order" or "for information" are not considered motions in the Bowling Contests. The member simply "calls for a division" when he desires a "division" and that is all there is to it. He does not go to the front of the room to hold a division placard and he suffers no penalty for calling for a division. The same is true of rising to a point of order or for information.

Lesson X

PARLIAMENTARY STRATEGY AND THE MOTION TO POSTPONE INDEFINITELY

The motion to postpone indefinitely is not a useful motion from the standpoint of its direct effect because it is just as easy to vote down the main motion as it is to pass the motion to postpone indefinitely since both are debatable and both have the lowest possible precedence. The real value of the motion to postpone indefinitely is strategic. *It is the motion by which the opposition to a motion or bill can ascertain the number of members in favor of the main motion without the risk of having the main motion adopted.*

If a member of the club should move that the members be assessed one dollar each so as to have ample funds in the club treasury, those opposed to this assessment should move at once to postpone consideration of this assessment indefinitely. Then, when debate is called for, they should present all of their arguments against the assessment. When the vote is finally taken on the motion to postpone indefinitely, the opposition to the assessment are in the position of advantage. If the motion to postpone indefinitely is carried, the motion to assess each member one dollar is "thrown out" and cannot be brought up again at that meeting. On the other hand, if the motion to postpone indefinitely is defeated, the opponents of the assessment still have the advantage of having learned how large a majority are in favor of the assessment, thus enabling the opponents of the assessment to determine just how many members now in favor of the assessment must be won over to the opposition in order to defeat the main motion when it comes up for final vote. Or, failing to swing enough votes over to the opposition, the opponents of the assessment can plan a campaign of delay (filibuster) to prevent a final vote at that session. As a last resort, when the opposition see that they are going to be defeated on the final vote, they can seek a compromise by amending the main motion so as to reduce the assessment to ten cents, or thirty cents or sixty cents.

In short, the motion to postpone indefinitely is the strategic motion used by the opposition to reveal the strength of the advocates of the main motion without the risk of having the main motion adopted. Having secured this information the leaders of the opposition are better able to plan their political campaign against the final passage of the main motion.

However, thorough discipline among the majority supporting the bill largely nullifies the effect of such strategic manoevers by the opposition. A capable leader with a well-disciplined army is not bothered by ambuscades or surprise attacks.

In winning the support of an undecided group,—one not already divided into two distinct factions,—both those for and those against a motion should realize that conduct, tone of voice and charm of personality are quite as important as good reasoning and forceful speaking.

Persons are not machines. On the contrary, they are ambitious, sometimes dignified, sometimes filled with a deep sense of what they consider right or wrong. How best to influence a group of people—be they boys or girls, men or women,—is something each person must work out for himself.

Some leaders impress their audience with their dignity, others with their humor,—still others win the audience with their forceful arguments. But all groups cannot be addressed in the same way.

A good leader must be able to "feel" the moods and whims of his audience but he must not respond too much. If he responds too much, he ceases to be a leader and becomes a follower. If he responds too little he soon finds himself a leader without followers.

One purpose of group leadership lessons and contests is to teach the aggressive student to become conscious of the desires and feelings of his audience and at the same time teach the timid student that every group demands some forcefulness and originality from its leader.

One of the charms of a great personality is naturalness,—the ability to be one's self. This does not mean, however, that you must consider yourself and your ideas perfect, nor that your friends must accept your ideas just because they are yours.

The leader must be able to judge his audience. He must know when to be reserved and dignified, when to be humorous, and when to be forceful.

Leadership and the group are not two separate things. They are merely two sides of the same thing. The leader is not effective without the group. The group to be effective must have leadership.

FREE FOR ALL CONTEST

The purpose of this contest is to train leaders to handle the fight for and against a measure when the line-up of the assembly for and against the original motion is unknown. Three students are appointed to make and support a motion of their own choosing. Three other students are appointed to oppose whatever motion is made. The remainder of the class are free to vote as they see fit. A time limit of fifteen minutes should be set for this contest.

If the "motion leader" is clever, he will formulate a motion which the assembly will want to pass. The "opposition leader" on the other hand, will attempt to change the motion by amendments which the assembly will favor. The assembly is the last court of appeal; consequently, the contest consists of a series of appeals to the likes and dislikes of the assembly, the method of the appeal being through the instrumentality of parliamentary procedure.

Chairman:—"THE MEETING WILL COME TO ORDER. IS THERE ANY BUSINESS?"

Motion Leader:—"MR. CHAIRMAN."

Chairman:—"MR. MOTION LEADER."

Motion Leader:—"I MOVE THAT WE HAVE A HOLIDAY THIS AFTERNOON."

Motion Leader's Assistant calls out, "I SECOND THE MOTION."

Chairman:—"IT IS MOVED AND SECONDED THAT WE HAVE A HOLIDAY THIS AFTERNOON. IS THERE ANY DISCUSSION?"

Both Opposition and Motion Leaders arise and address the Chair:—"MR. CHAIRMAN," "MR. CHAIRMAN."

Chairman:—"MR. OPPOSITION LEADER." *(Chairman recognizes Opposition Leader because Motion Leader has just "had the floor".)*

Opposition Leader:—"THIS MOTION CONTAINS A GOOD IDEA. WE ALL LIKE HOLIDAYS. BUT THIS MOTION WAS MADE UP WITHOUT REGARD FOR THE WISHES OF THIS ASSEMBLY. APPARENTLY NO ATTEMPT WAS MADE TO ASCERTAIN WHETHER THIS AFTERNOON WOULD BE ANY BETTER FOR A HOLIDAY THAN TOMORROW AFTERNOON. THERE IS NO SPECIAL REASON FOR A HOLIDAY THIS AFTERNOON, WHEREAS TOMORROW AFTERNOON THERE IS TO BE A BASKETBALL GAME THAT WE WOULD ALL LIKE TO ATTEND. BECAUSE THE MOTION WAS MADE WITHOUT ANY REGARD FOR THE WISHES OF THE ASSEMBLY, I MOVE THAT WE POSTPONE CONSIDERATION OF THIS MOTION INDEFINITELY."

Opposition Leader's Assistant calls out, "I SECOND THE MOTION."

Chairman:—"IT IS MOVED AND SECONDED THAT WE POSTPONE CONSIDERATION OF THIS MOTION INDEFINITELY. IS THERE ANY DISCUSSION?"

Motion Leader and Opposition Leader:—"MR. CHAIRMAN." "MR. CHAIRMAN."

Chairman:—"MR. MOTION LEADER." *(Chairman recognizes Motion Leader this time, because Opposition Leader had the floor last.)*

Motion Leader:—"I MOVE THAT WE CLOSE DEBATE AND VOTE IMMEDIATELY ON THE PENDING QUESTION."

Motion Leader's Assistant calls out, "I SECOND THE MOTION."

Chairman:—"IT IS MOVED AND SECONDED THAT WE CLOSE DEBATE AND VOTE IMMEDIATELY ON THE PENDING QUESTION, WHICH IS THE MOTION TO POSTPONE INDEFINITELY. THOSE IN FAVOR OF THE MOTION TO CLOSE DEBATE SAY 'I'." *(Many vote "I".)* "THOSE OPPOSED SAY 'NO'." *(A few vote "No".)*

Chairman:—"THE 'I's' HAVE IT."

Opposition Leader:—"I CALL FOR A DIVISION."

Chairman:—"A DIVISION OF VOTE HAS BEEN CALLED FOR. THOSE IN FAVOR OF THE MOTION TO CLOSE DEBATE RAISE THEIR RIGHT HAND." *(20 raise their hand.)* "THOSE OPPOSED TO THE MOTION TO CLOSE DEBATE RAISE THEIR HAND." *(9 raise their hand.)*

Chairman:—"THE VOTE IS 20 FOR AND 9 AGAINST. THE 'I's' HAVE IT BY A TWO-THIRDS VOTE AND THE MOTION TO CLOSE DEBATE IS CARRIED. THE NEXT BUSINESS IS THE VOTE ON THE MOTION TO POSTPONE CONSIDERATION INDEFINITELY. THOSE IN FAVOR OF THE MOTION TO POSTPONE INDEFINITELY SAY 'I'." *(11 vote "I".)* "THOSE OPPOSED SAY 'NO'." *(18 vote "No.")*

(Presumably the large majority of the assembly want a holiday, but the opposition group of three and eight of their friends vote in favor of the motion to postpone indefinitely simply because they want Opposition Leader to win.)

Chairman:—"THE 'NOES' HAVE IT AND THE MOTION TO POSTPONE INDEFINITELY IS LOST. IS THERE ANY FURTHER DISCUSSION ON THE MOTION TO HAVE A HOLIDAY THIS AFTERNOON?"

Opposition Leader:—"MR. CHAIRMAN."

Chairman:—"MR. OPPOSITION LEADER."

Opposition Leader:—"WHILE IT IS EVIDENT THAT THE ASSEMBLY DESIRES A HOLIDAY THIS AFTERNOON, I AM SURE THAT THEY WOULD RATHER HAVE A HOLIDAY ALL DAY TOMORROW. THEREFORE I MOVE THAT WE AMEND THE MOTION BY STRIKING OUT THE WORDS 'THIS AFTERNOON' AND ADDING THE WORD 'TOMORROW'."

Opposition Leader's Assistant calls out, "I SECOND THE MOTION."

Chairman:—"IT IS MOVED AND SECONDED THAT WE AMEND THE MOTION BY STRIKING OUT THE WORDS 'THIS AFTERNOON' AND ADDING THE WORD 'TOMORROW,' SO THAT THE MOTION IF AMENDED WILL READ, THAT WE HAVE A HOLIDAY TOMORROW. IS THERE ANY DISCUSSION ON THE AMENDMENT?"

Motion Leader:—"MR. CHAIRMAN, I RISE FOR A PARLIAMENTARY INQUIRY."

Chairman:—"STATE YOUR INQUIRY."

Motion Leader:—"DOES NOT THE MOTION TO CLOSE DEBATE CUT OFF AMENDMENTS?"

Chairman:—"IT DOES CUT OFF AMENDMENTS TO THE MOTION TO WHICH IT APPLIES. HOWEVER, YOUR MOTION TO CLOSE DEBATE APPLIED ONLY TO THE MOTION TO POSTPONE INDEFINITELY. IF YOU DESIRED TO CUT OFF AMENDMENTS TO ALL PENDING MOTIONS YOU SHOULD HAVE MOVED TO CLOSE DEBATE ON ALL PENDING QUESTIONS."

Motion Leader:—"VERY WELL. I MOVE THAT WE CLOSE DEBATE AND VOTE IMMEDIATELY ON *ALL* PENDING QUESTIONS."

Motion Leader's Assistant calls out, "I SECOND THE MOTION."

Chairman:—"IT IS MOVED AND SECONDED THAT WE CLOSE DEBATE AND VOTE IMMEDIATELY ON *ALL* PENDING QUESTIONS. THOSE IN FAVOR OF THE MOTION TO CLOSE DEBATE ON ALL PENDING QUESTIONS PLEASE RAISE THEIR RIGHT HAND." *(22 raise their hand)* "THOSE OPPOSED PLEASE RAISE THEIR RIGHT HAND." *(8 raise their hand.)*

Note:—Some of the opposition vote "I" because they think the amendment will carry and thus win the contest for the opposition leader. However, the opposition leader votes "No" because he is afraid to risk all on the success of the amendment. If the amendment is lost after the motion to close debate on all pending questions is carried, then the opposition leader will not be able to offer any other amendments.

Chairman:—"THE VOTE IS 22 FOR AND 8 AGAINST. THE 'I's' HAVE IT BY A TWO-THIRDS VOTE AND THE MOTION TO CLOSE DEBATE ON ALL PENDING QUESTIONS IS CARRIED. THE NEXT BUSINESS IS THE VOTE ON THE AMENDMENT THAT WE STRIKE OUT THE WORDS 'THIS AFTERNOON' AND INSERT THE WORD 'TOMORROW'. THOSE IN FAVOR OF THE AMENDMENT SAY 'I'." *(Many vote "I".)* "THOSE OPPOSED SAY 'NO'." *(Quite a few vote "No.")*

Chairman:—"THE CHAIR IS IN DOUBT. THOSE IN FAVOR OF THE AMENDMENT PLEASE RAISE THEIR RIGHT HAND." *(16 raise their hand.)* "THOSE OPPOSED RAISE THEIR HAND." *(14 raise their hand.)*

Chairman: — "THE VOTE IS 'I's' 16, 'NOES' 14. THE 'I's' HAVE IT AND THE AMENDMENT IS CARRIED. THE NEXT BUSINESS IS THE VOTE ON THE MOTION AS AMENDED WHICH READS THAT WE HAVE A HOLIDAY TOMORROW. THOSE IN FAVOR OF THE MOTION AS AMENDED SAY 'I'." *(Many vote "I".)* "THOSE OPPOSED SAY 'NO'." *(Quite a few vote "No".)*

Motion Leader:—"I CALL FOR A DIVISION."

Chairman:—"A DIVISION HAS BEEN CALLED FOR. THOSE IN FAVOR OF THE MOTION AS AMENDED PLEASE RISE. *(24 stand up.)* BE SEATED. THOSE OPPOSED PLEASE RISE. *(6 stand up.)* BE SEATED."

Chairman:—"THE VOTE IS 'I's' 24, 'NOES' 6. THE 'I's' HAVE IT AND THE MOTION AS AMENDED IS CARRIED. IS THERE ANY OTHER BUSINESS?"

Opposition Leader:—"MR. CHAIRMAN."

Chairman:—"MR. OPPOSITION LEADER."

Opposition Leader:—"I MOVE THAT WE ADJOURN."

Opposition Leader's Assistant calls out, "I SECOND THE MOTION."

Chairman:—"IT IS MOVED AND SECONDED THAT WE ADJOURN. THOSE IN FAVOR OF ADJOURNMENT SAY 'I'." *(Assembly votes many "I's".)* "THOSE OPPOSED SAY 'NO'." *(Only a few vote "No.")*

Chairman:—"THE 'I's' HAVE IT AND THE MOTION TO ADJOURN IS CARRIED. YOU STAND ADJOURNED." *(Sounds gavel.)*

The opposition wins this contest because the rule is that the group that makes the motion must get it passed within the time limit and *without any change* in the original motion. Ordinarily the opposition should win this free for all contest because the opposition can do so many things to delay action and suggest so many different amendments to change the motion, whereas the motion leader can do very little to speed up action and prevent amendments unless he has a two-thirds majority to close debate and cut off amendments. It is seldom that either side can command a two-thirds majority in this "free for all" type of contest.

PERSUASION, COMPROMISE AND REBELLION

In this dramatized contest the minority does not use every possible method of delay, because such extreme obstruction methods would probably so antagonize the chairman and the majority as to cause them to ignore the legitimate rights of the minority.

Self-government is based absolutely upon mutual concession. A tyrannical, unreasonable minority is just as bad as a tyrannical, unreasonable majority. The oft-repeated assertion that "the majority is always wrong" is just a conceited statement of self-praise by the minority. No group is always right or always wrong. The very purpose of a deliberative assembly is to arrive at the truth, at least to arrive at a wise compromise by considering the arguments of every side of the question represented in the assembly. The chairman should protect the rights of the minority for two reasons, first, to insure that the majority hear arguments both for and against the motion before it is adopted in order that the assembly may act only after hearing all sides of the question. The second reason for protecting the rights of the minority is to make the minority better satisfied, or more willing to abide by the decision of the majority.

Revolution is the result of tyranny of a minority. A minority gets into a position of legal advantage where it can prevent the majority from having its way in a legal manner. Consequently, the majority, conscious of its real power, uses illegal methods to overthrow this legally intrenched minority.

Rebellion, on the other hand, is the result of the tyranny of a majority. The majority, conscious of its superior numbers, becomes tyrannical and ignores the rights of the minority. And since liberty-loving citizens will fight for their liberty, this minority, denied its legal right to be heard, uses illegal methods of violence to express its opposition to the tyranny of the majority.

In brief, self-government is a political habit that may be learned by much practice. It is the habit of government by and after discussion, in other words, government by public opinion. In such a government certain persons are always in the minority because of their temperament. They are always "against the crowd", "agin' the government". They habitually think negatively. Other persons of different temperament are always "with the crowd", "for the government". One small group believes that the majoritiy is always right. Another small group believes that the majority is always wrong.

Fortunately, most people are open to persuasion on most subjects and are willing to listen to the arguments for and against every proposal in order that they may act wisely in opposing or supporting every proposal made. It is this last group that really determines the policy of every group, township, city, county, state or nation. It is this group that is open to persuasion that makes self-government workable, because they are the group that decides wisely after hearing the arguments from both sides.

Self-government must fail when policies must be decided arbitrarily by some small group simply because most of the citizens do not know how to be effective in a self-governing group. Tyranny is the inevitable result of the ignorance and neglect of the great mass of the citizenry.

Students can learn the art of self-government by practicing year after year to govern their own groups through discussion and through the compromise of conflicting interests.

Lesson XI

MOTION TO RECONSIDER

The motion to reconsider is the most difficult of all motions if one takes into account all of its technical phases. However, it is not used frequently, and when it is used there is seldom occasion for using its more difficult phases.

Like the motion to amend, the motion to reconsider is an appendage motion, that is to say, it takes its rank or precedence from the motion to which it applies. It is debatable when the motion to which it applies is debatable. A subsidiary motion must, as a rule, be reconsidered, if at all, immediately after the vote on that subsidiary motion has been decided and before any other motion is moved. (This rule does not apply, however, to reconsideration of the motion to amend.)

The technical difficulties involved in the motion to reconsider are first, that it can be moved and seconded only by those who voted with the prevailing side whenever it is definitely known who did vote on each side. Second, it is in order to move reconsideration only for a short period after the vote was taken on the motion to be reconsidered. This period is usually one legislative day. Third, because the motion to reconsider must be moved within a fixed, brief period after the vote on the motion to be reconsidered, it is permissable to interrupt another member who has the floor in order to move reconsideration before the time for moving reconsideration expires.

Fourth, the high privilege accorded the motion to reconsider for entry, that is for moving it, does not extend to the discussion or vote on the motion to reconsider. To illustrate:— If a main motion to raise the dues were voted on yesterday and adopted, and the time for today's session had almost expired, one of those who voted for its adoption yesterday could interrupt another member who had the floor in order to move reconsideration of the vote on the motion to raise the dues. However, no action could be taken on this motion "to reconsider the vote on the motion to raise the dues" until there was nothing else before the assembly, because for discussion and vote the motion to reconsider has the rank or precedence only of the motion to which it applies. This motion to raise the dues was a main motion, consequently, the "motion to reconsider the vote on the motion to raise the dues" has the precedence of a main motion only and that precedence is the lowest of all, that is, it can be brought before the assembly for discussion and vote only when there is no other business before the assembly.

A final complication of the motion to reconsider is that when moved it automatically suspends action on the motion to which it applies until the motion to reconsider has been acted on.

Thus by interrupting another member before the close of to-day's session and moving reconsideration of the vote on the motion to raise the dues, the raising of the dues is suspended until a vote can be taken on the "motion to reconsider the vote on the motion to raise the dues."

CLINCHING A MOTION

Because of the possibility that some member of the majority may change his mind over night and then move reconsideration tomorrow to stop action on the motion to raise the dues, it is a common parliamentary trick for the majority leader to move reconsideration just as soon as the main motion is adopted. Then the majority *votes down* the motion to reconsider. In this way the passage of the main motion is "clinched" (made secure), because no motion may be twice reconsidered.

Of course, what is sauce for the goose is sauce for the gander. While the privilege of moving to reconsider pertains only to those who voted with the prevailing side, there is nothing to keep a member of the opposition from voting with the majority for the sole purpose of qualifying himself to move reconsideration. By this strategy the opposition may use the motion to reconsider as one of the many ways of delaying final action on the main motion. This is especially effective obstructionist tactics because of the fact that nearly all subsidiary motions may be reconsidered, and, therefore, by this reconsideration strategy the opposition may require two votes on almost every subsidiary motion, as well as on the main motion. (See block 1 in chart under motion to reconsider, page 19 in manual.)

The following exercise illustrates the simpler uses of the motion to reconsider.

This is in the form of a majority-minority contest with the majority having a two-thirds vote.

Chairman:—"THE MEETING WILL COME TO ORDER. IS THERE ANY BUSINESS?"

Majority Leader:—"MR. CHAIRMAN."

Chairman:—"MR. MAJORITY LEADER."

Majority Leader:—"I MOVE THAT WE RAISE THE ANNUAL DUES OF THIS ORGANIZATION TO FIVE DOLLARS."

Chairman:—"IS THERE A SECOND TO THIS MOTION?"

Majority Leader's Assistant:—"I SECOND THE MOTION."

Chairman:—"IT IS MOVED AND SECONDED THAT WE RAISE THE ANNUAL DUES TO FIVE DOLLARS. IS THERE ANY DISCUSSION?"

Minority Leader:—"MR. CHAIRMAN."

Chairman:—"MR. MINORITY LEADER."

Minority Leader:—"THIS RAISING OF THE DUES IS, IN MY OPINION, VERY UNWISE. FEW MEMBERS CAN AFFORD TO PAY FIVE DOLLARS AND THE ORGANIZATION DOES NOT NEED THIS MUCH MONEY. THEREFORE, I MOVE THAT THE CONSIDERATION OF THIS MOTION BE POSTPONED INDEFINITELY."

Minority Leader's Assistant:—"I SECOND THE MOTION."

Chairman:—"IT IS MOVED AND SECONDED THAT WE POSTPONE CONSIDERATION OF THIS MOTION INDEFINITELY. IS THERE ANY DISCUSSION?"

Majority Leader:—"MR. CHAIRMAN."

Chairman:—"MR. MAJORITY LEADER."

Majority Leader:—"I BEG TO DIFFER WITH THE LAST SPEAKER. ANY MEMBER CAN AFFORD TO PAY FIVE DOLLARS A YEAR FOR THE SPLENDID FACILITIES OF THIS ORGANIZATION AND THE ORGANIZATION DOES NEED THE ADDITIONAL FUNDS WHICH THIS INCREASE IN DUES WILL PROVIDE. I MOVE THAT WE CLOSE DEBATE AND VOTE IMMEDIATELY ON THE PENDING QUESTION."

Majority Leader's Assistant:—"I SECOND THE MOTION."

Chairman:—"IT IS MOVED AND SECONDED THAT WE CLOSE DEBATE AND VOTE IMMEDIATELY ON THE PENDING QUESTION. THOSE IN FAVOR OF THE MOTION TO CLOSE DEBATE PLEASE RAISE THE RIGHT HAND." (20 raise their hand.) "THOSE OPPOSED PLEASE RAISE THE RIGHT HAND." (9 raise their hand.)

Chairman:—"THE VOTE IS 20 FOR AND 9 AGAINST. THE 'I's' HAVE IT BY A TWO-THIRDS VOTE AND THE MOTION TO CLOSE DEBATE IS CARRIED. THE NEXT BUSINESS IS THE VOTE ON THE MOTION TO POSTPONE INDEFINITELY. THOSE IN FAVOR OF POSTPONING CONSIDERATION OF THIS MOTION INDEFINITELY SAY 'I'." (Many vote "I".) "THOSE OPPOSED SAY 'NO'." (A few vote "No.")

Minority Leader:—"I CALL FOR A DIVISION OF VOTE."

Chairman:—"A DIVISION OF VOTE IS CALLED FOR. THOSE IN FAVOR OF THE MOTION TO POSTPONE INDEFINITELY PLEASE STAND." (10 stand up.) "BE SEATED. THOSE OPPOSED TO INDEFINITE POST-

PONEMENT PLEASE STAND." *(19 stand up.)* "BE SEATED."

Chairman:—"THE VOTE IS 10 FOR AND 19 AGAINST. THE 'NOES' HAVE IT AND THE MOTION TO POSTPONE INDEFINITELY IS LOST. IS THERE ANY FURTHER DISCUSSION ON THE MOTION TO RAISE THE DUES TO FIVE DOLLARS?"

Minority Leader:—"MR. CHAIRMAN."

Chairman:—"MR. MINORITY LEADER."

Minority Leader:—"I MOVE THAT WE AMEND THE MOTION BY STRIKING OUT THE NUMBER '5' AND INSERTING THE NUMBER '4'."

Minority Leader's Assistant:—"I SECOND THE MOTION."

Chairman:—"IT IS MOVED AND SECONDED THAT WE AMEND THE ORIGINAL MOTION BY STRIKING OUT THE NUMBER '5' AND INSERTING THE NUMBER '4', SO THAT THE MAIN MOTION, IF AMENDED, WILL READ THAT WE RAISE THE ANNUAL DUES TO 4 DOLLARS. IS THERE ANY DISCUSSION ON THE AMENDMENT?"

Majority Leader:—"MR. CHAIRMAN."

Chairman:—"MR. MAJORITY LEADER."

Majority Leader:—"FOUR DOLLARS WILL NOT PROVIDE ENOUGH MONEY FOR THE PROGRAM WE HAVE PLANNED FOR NEXT YEAR. OUR BUDGET FOR NEXT YEAR IS BASED UPON ANNUAL DUES OF FIVE DOLLARS. EITHER WE MUST RAISE THE DUES TO FIVE DOLLARS, OR ELSE WE MUST ABANDON OUR ENLARGED PROGRAM FOR NEXT YEAR. I AM CONVINCED THAT THE OVERWHELMING MAJORITY OF THE MEMBERS ARE IN FAVOR OF RAISING THE DUES TO FIVE DOLLARS."

Minority Leader:—"MR. CHAIRMAN."

Chairman:—"MR. MINORITY LEADER."

Minority Leader:—"THE LAST SPEAKER MAY BE CORRECT IN SAYING THAT THE MAJORITY OF THE MEMBERS FAVOR ANNUAL DUES OF FIVE DOLLARS. BUT THOSE FEW OF US WHO CAN NOT AFFORD TO PAY FIVE DOLLARS WISH TO RAISE THE POINT THAT FOUR DOLLARS A YEAR FROM ALL OF THE PRESENT MEMBERS MAY BRING IN MORE MONEY THAN FIVE DOLLARS DUES FROM THE SMALLER NUMBER WHO CAN PAY THE FIVE DOLLARS. RAISING THE DUES IS ONE WAY OF FORC-

ING THE POORER MEMBERS OUT OF THE CLUB. IF THAT IS THE PURPOSE, VERY WELL, WE CAN RESIGN FROM THE CLUB. I AM AMENDING THE MOTION SO THAT THOSE OF US WHO ARE NOT SO PROSPEROUS MAY BE ABLE TO CONTINUE OUR MEMBERSHIP IN THE CLUB."

Majority Leader:—"MR. CHAIRMAN."

Chairman:—"MR. MAJORITY LEADER."

Majority Leader:—"I AM SURE THAT THERE IS NO DESIRE TO FORCE ANY MEMBER OUT OF THE CLUB. NOR DO I BELIEVE THAT THE DIFFERENCE OF ONE DOLLAR WILL CAUSE ANY ONE TO RESIGN FROM THE CLUB. BUT IT IS TRUE THAT MINORITIES SOMETIMES ATTEMPT TO RUN ORGANIZATIONS AGAINST THE MANIFEST DESIRES OF THE MAJORITY. I BELIEVE THAT THE POINT AT ISSUE HAS BEEN DISCUSSED SUFFICIENTLY. THEREFORE, I MOVE THAT WE CLOSE DEBATE AND VOTE IMMEDIATELY ON *ALL* PENDING QUESTIONS."

Majority Leader's Assistant:—"I SECOND THE MOTION."

Chairman:—"IT IS MOVED AND SECONDED THAT WE CLOSE DEBATE AND VOTE IMMEDIATELY ON *ALL* PENDING QUESTIONS. THOSE IN FAVOR—" (Interruption.)

(Note: Minority Leader interrupts rather angrily because he is now convinced that the majority are going to "steam-roll" the minority. For this reason Minority Leader feels justified in obstructing in every way that he can.)

Minority Leader:—(angrily)—"MR. CHAIRMAN, I RISE FOR A PARLIAMENTARY INQUIRY."

Chairman:—"STATE YOUR INQUIRY."

Minority Leader:—"IS THE MOTION 'TO TABLE' IN ORDER AT THIS TIME?"

Chairman:—"IT IS."

Minority Leader:—"THEN I MOVE THAT THIS ENTIRE QUESTION BE LAID ON THE TABLE."

Minority Leader's Assistant:—"I SECOND THE MOTION."

Chairman:—"IT IS MOVED AND SECONDED THAT WE LAY ON THE TABLE THIS ENTIRE QUESTION OF A RAISE IN DUES. THOSE IN FAVOR OF TABLING THIS ENTIRE QUESTION SAY 'I'." *(A few vote 'I'.)* "THOSE OPPOSED SAY 'NO'." *(Many vote "No.")*

Minority Leader:—"I CALL FOR A DIVISION."

Chairman:—"THOSE IN FAVOR OF TABLING THIS QUES-TION OF RAISING THE DUES PLEASE STAND." *(9 stand up.)* "BE SEATED. THOSE OPPOSED PLEASE STAND." *(16 stand up.)*

Chairman:—"THE VOTE IS 9 FOR AND 16 AGAINST. THE 'NOES' HAVE IT AND THE MOTION TO TABLE IS LOST. THE NEXT BUSINESS IS THE VOTE ON THE MOTION TO CLOSE DEBATE. THOSE IN FAVOR OF CLOSING DEBATE ON *ALL* PENDING QUESTIONS PLEASE RAISE THE RIGHT HAND. *(20 raise their hand. When Minority Leader sees that two-thirds of the assembly are voting to close debate, he and his assistant raise their hands, making 22 all together.)*

Chairman:—(Continuing the vote)—"THOSE OPPOSED TO CLOSING DEBATE ON ALL PENDING QUESTIONS PLEASE RAISE THE RIGHT HAND." *(7 raise their hand.)*

Chairman:—"THE VOTE IS 22 FOR AND 7 AGAINST. THE 'I's' HAVE IT BY A TWO-THIRDS VOTE AND THE MOTION TO CLOSE DEBATE ON *ALL* PENDING QUESTIONS IS CARRIED." (Interruption again.)

Minority Leader:—"MR. CHAIRMAN."

Chairman:—"MR. MINORITY LEADER."

Minority Leader:—"I MOVE THAT WE RECONSIDER THE VOTE ON THE MOTION TO CLOSE DEBATE."

Minority Leader's Assistant:—"I SECOND THE MOTION."

Chairman:—"DID YOU VOTE WITH THE PREVAILING SIDE?"

Minority Leader:—"WE DID."

Chairman:—"IT IS MOVED AND SECONDED THAT WE RECONSIDER THE VOTE ON THE MOTION TO CLOSE DEBATE ON ALL PENDING QUESTIONS. THOSE IN FAVOR OF THE MOTION TO RECON-SIDER PLEASE RAISE THE RIGHT HAND." *(9 raise their hand.)* "THOSE OPPOSED TO RECONSIDERA-TION PLEASE RAISE THE RIGHT HAND." *(20 raise their hand.)*

Chairman:—"THE VOTE IS 9 FOR AND 20 AGAINST. THE 'NOES' HAVE IT AND THE MOTION TO RECON-SIDER IS LOST. THE NEXT BUSINESS IS THE VOTE ON THE AMENDMENT THAT WE STRIKE OUT THE NUMBER '5' AND INSERT THE NUMBER '4'. THOSE IN FAVOR OF THE AMENDMENT SAY 'I'."

(A few vote "I".) "THOSE OPPOSED SAY 'NO'." *(Many vote "No.")*

Chairman:—"THE 'NOES' SEEM TO HAVE IT."

Minority Leader:—"I CALL FOR A DIVISION OF VOTE."

Chairman:—"A DIVISION OF VOTE IS CALLED FOR. THOSE IN FAVOR OF THE AMENDMENT PLEASE STAND." *(9 stand up.)* "BE SEATED. THOSE OPPOSED TO THE AMENDMENT PLEASE STAND." *(20 stand up.)*

Chairman:—"THE VOTE IS 9 FOR AND 20 AGAINST. THE 'NOES' HAVE IT AND THE AMENDMENT IS LOST. THE NEXT BUSINESS IS—" (Interruption.)

Minority Leader:—"MR. CHAIRMAN."

Chairman:—"MR. MINORITY LEADER."

Minority Leader:—"I MOVE THAT WE ADJOURN."

Minority Leader's Assistant:—"I SECOND THE MOTION."

Chairman:—"IT IS MOVED AND SECONDED THAT WE ADJOURN. THOSE IN FAVOR OF ADJOURNMENT SAY 'I'." *(A few vote "I".)* "THOSE OPPOSED SAY 'NO'," *(Many vote "No.")*

Chairman:—"THE 'NOES' HAVE IT AND THE MOTION TO ADJOURN IS LOST. THE NEXT BUSINESS IS THE VOTE ON THE MOTION TO RAISE THE ANNUAL DUES TO FIVE DOLLARS. THOSE IN FAVOR—" (Interruption.)

Minority Leader:—"MR. CHAIRMAN, I RISE FOR A PARLIAMENTARY INQUIRY."

Chairman:—(a bit impatiently)—"STATE YOUR INQUIRY."

Minority Leader:—"IS NOT THIS MOTION DEBATABLE?"

Chairman:—"NOT NOW, BECAUSE THE MOTION TO CLOSE DEBATE ON ALL PENDING QUESTIONS WAS CARRIED."

Minority Leader:—"ARE AMENDMENTS IN ORDER NOW?"

Chairman:—"NO, THE MOTION TO CLOSE DEBATE ALSO CUTS OFF ANY FURTHER AMENDMENT OF THE MOTION TO WHICH IT APPLIES. THE VOTE IS NOW ON THE ORIGINAL MOTION THAT WE RAISE THE ANNUAL DUES TO FIVE DOLLARS. THOSE IN FAVOR OF THIS MOTION PLEASE STAND." *(22 stand up, including the minority leader and his assistant.)* "THOSE OPPOSED PLEASE STAND." *(7 stand up.)*

Chairman:—"THE VOTE IS 22 FOR AND 7 AGAINST. THE 'I's' HAVE IT AND THE MOTION TO RAISE THE ANNUAL DUES TO FIVE DOLLARS IS CARRIED. IS THERE ANY FURTHER BUSINESS?"

Both Majority and Minority Leaders address the Chair:—"MR. CHAIRMAN. MR. CHAIRMAN."

Chairman:—"MR. MAJORITY LEADER."

Majority Leader:—"THIS INCREASE IN DUES SHOULD BECOME EFFECTIVE AT ONCE, BECAUSE SOME NEW MEMBERS ARE JOINING THE CLUB TODAY. IT IS MY DESIRE TO 'CLINCH' THIS MOTION BY MOVING RECONSIDERATION AND THEN VOTING DOWN THE MOTION TO RECONSIDER. THEREFORE, I MOVE RECONSIDERATION OF THE VOTE ON THE MOTION TO RAISE THE DUES TO FIVE DOLLARS."

Majority Leader's Assistant:—"I SECOND THE MOTION."

Chairman:—"IT IS MOVED AND SECONDED THAT WE RECONSIDER THE VOTE ON THE MOTION TO RAISE THE DUES TO FIVE DOLLARS. IS THERE ANY DISCUSSION ON THE MOTION TO RECONSIDER?"

Minority Leader:—"MR. CHAIRMAN."

Chairman:—"MR. MINORITY LEADER."

Minority Leader:—"THE ACTION OF THE MAJORITY LEADER ONLY CONFIRMS MY STATEMENT THAT HE IS DETERMINED TO HAVE HIS WAY REGARDLESS OF THE FACT THAT SOME OF THE MEMBERS OF THE CLUB ARE NOT HERE TONIGHT TO EXPRESS THEIR DISAPPROVAL OF BOOSTING THE ANNUAL DUES TO FIVE DOLLARS. IT IS MY SINCERE OPINION THAT THIS MATTER SHOULD NOT BE IRREVOCABLY SETTLED TONIGHT. IT SHOULD BE LEFT OPEN UNTIL THE NEXT MEETING WHEN ALL OF THE MEMBERS CAN BE INFORMED OF THIS RAISE OF DUES AND BE GIVEN OPPORTUNITY TO EXPRESS THEMSELVES ABOUT IT. THEREFORE, I MOVE THAT THE VOTE ON THIS MOTION TO RECONSIDER BE POSTPONED UNTIL THE NEXT REGULAR MEETING."

Minority Leader's Assistant:—"I SECOND THE MOTION."

Chairman:—"IT IS MOVED AND SECONDED THAT WE POSTPONE FINAL ACTION ON THIS MOTION TO RECONSIDER UNTIL THE NEXT REGULAR MEETING. IS THERE ANY DISCUSSION AS TO THE ADVISABILITY OF POSTPONEMENT?"

Majority Leader:—"MR. CHAIRMAN."

Chairman:—"MR. MAJORITY LEADER."

Majority Leader:—"THE VOTE OF 22 TO 7 IS SUFFICIENT INDICATION OF THE APPROVAL OF THIS RAISE IN DUES BY THREE-FOURTHS OF THE MEMBERS OF THE CLUB. I MOVE THAT WE CLOSE DEBATE AND VOTE IMMEDIATELY ON *ALL* PENDING QUESTIONS."

Majority Leader's Assistant:—"I SECOND THE MOTION."

Chairman:—"IT IS MOVED AND SECONDED THAT WE CLOSE DEBATE AND VOTE IMMEDIATELY ON *ALL* PENDING QUESTIONS. THOSE IN FAVOR OF CLOSING DEBATE ON *ALL* PENDING QUESTIONS PLEASE RAISE THE RIGHT HAND." *(20 raise their hand.)* "THOSE OPPOSED PLEASE RAISE THE RIGHT HAND." *(9 raise their hand.)*

Chairman:—"THE VOTE IS 20 FOR AND 9 AGAINST. THE MOTION TO CLOSE DEBATE ON ALL PENDING QUESTIONS IS CARRIED."—(Interruption.)

Minority Leader:—"MR. CHAIRMAN."

Chairman:—(impatiently)—"MR. MINORITY LEADER."

Minority Leader:—"I MOVE THAT WE LAY THE MOTION TO RECONSIDER ON THE TABLE."

Minority Leader's Assistant:—"I SECOND THE MOTION."

Chairman:—"IT IS MOVED AND SECONDED THAT WE LAY THE MOTION TO RECONSIDER ON THE TABLE. THOSE IN FAVOR SAY 'I'." *(A few vote "I".)* "THOSE OPPOSED SAY 'NO'." *(Many vote "No.")*

Minority Leader:—"DIVISION!"

Chairman:—"THOSE IN FAVOR OF TABLING THE MOTION TO RECONSIDER PLEASE RAISE THE RIGHT HAND." *(9 raise their hand.)* "THOSE OPPOSED PLEASE RAISE THE RIGHT HAND." *(22 including the minority leader and his assistant raise their hand. It is entirely proper for any one to vote both for and against a motion. Of course, the effect is the same as not voting at all except that a person who does not vote at all can not move reconsideration.)*

Chairman:—"THE VOTE IS 9 FOR AND 22 AGAINST. THE MOTION TO TABLE IS LOST. THE NEXT BUSINESS IS—" (Interruption.)

Minority Leader:—"MR. CHAIRMAN."

Chairman:—(with impatience.) "MR. MINORITY LEADER."

Minority Leader:—"I MOVE THAT WE RECONSIDER THE VOTE ON THE MOTION TO TABLE."

Chairman:—"YOUR MOTION IS OUT OF ORDER. THE MOTION TO TABLE CAN NOT BE RECONSIDERED. THE NEXT BUSINESS IS THE VOTE ON THE MOTION TO POSTPONE CONSIDERATION OF THE MOTION TO RECONSIDER UNTIL THE NEXT MEETING. THOSE IN FAVOR OF POSTPONEMENT UNTIL THE NEXT MEETING SAY 'I'." *(A few vote "I".)* "THOSE OPPOSED SAY 'NO'." *(Many vote "No.")*

Minority Leader:—"DIVISION."

Chairman:—"THE VOTE IS ON THE MOTION TO POSTPONE CONSIDERATION OF THE MOTION TO RECONSIDER. THOSE IN FAVOR OF POSTPONING CONSIDERATION PLEASE STAND." *(9 stand.)* "BE SEATED. THOSE OPPOSED TO POSTPONEMENT PLEASE STAND." *(20 stand.)* "BE SEATED."

Chairman:—"THE 'NOES' HAVE IT BY A VOTE OF 20 TO 9. THE MOTION TO POSTPONE CONSIDERATION OF THE MOTION TO RECONSIDER IS LOST. THE NEXT BUSINESS IS THE VOTE ON THE MOTION TO RECONSIDER THE VOTE ON THE MOTION TO RAISE THE DUES. THOSE IN FAVOR OF RECONSIDERATION PLEASE STAND." *(9 stand.)* "BE SEATED. THOSE OPPOSED TO RECONSIDERATION PLEASE STAND." *(20 stand.)* "BE SEATED."

Chairman:—"THE VOTE IS 9 FOR AND 20 AGAINST. THE MOTION TO RECONSIDER IS LOST. IS THERE ANY OTHER BUSINESS?"

Majority Leader:—"MR. CHAIRMAN."

Chairman:—"MR. MAJORITY LEADER."

Majority Leader:—"I MOVE THAT WE ADJOURN."

Majority Leader's Assistant:—"I SECOND THE MOTION."

Chairman:—"IT IS MOVED AND SECONDED THAT WE ADJOURN. THOSE IN FAVOR SAY 'I'." *(Many vote "I".)* "THOSE OPPOSED SAY 'NO'." *(A few vote "No".)*

Chairman:—"THE 'I'S' HAVE IT AND THE MOTION TO ADJOURN IS CARRIED. YOU STAND ADJOURNED." *(Sounds gavel.)*

Some use of the motion to reconsider is necessary in order that mistakes may be corrected when discovered. But all the intricacies of the motion to reconsider are needed only in a legislative body that has a large membership and a tremendous mass of legislation to deal with.

Further delving into the intricacies of the motion to reconsider is not advisable for the purposes of an ordinary discussion group. A rapid reading of the rules that apply to the motion to reconsider as listed in Robert, Cushing, Luce, the Congressional Manual or other standard work on parliamentary procedure will make it clear that no one but a research student in the field can pretend to master all the intricacies of this appendage motion which has a different precedence for each motion to which it applies and, worse still, has one precedence for entry and another for reconsideration and vote.

For the student who likes to master every subject he takes up, it is well to remember that the final authority on procedure in the United States is the twelve large volumes of Hind's "Precedents", and that even these precedents are being modified by every session of Congress, since the complete authority of Congress to determine its own procedure is guaranteed by the United States Constitution. ("Each House may determine the rules of its proceedings, ... " Art. I, section 5, second paragraph.)

This manual gives, for obvious reasons, only the simpler phases of the motion to reconsider. The instructor should call attention to the fact that item 8 (last one on the right hand page) in the chart under the motion to reconsider (page 19 in manual) tells what motions may apply to the motion to reconsider. Also item 1 (the first one on the left hand page) in this chart tells what motions may be reconsidered.

It should also be noted at this point that the motion to lay on the table may not be reconsidered for the obvious reason that the motion to take from the table accomplishes the same result after an "I" vote on the motion to table. Reconsideration of a "No" vote on the motion to table is unnecessary because the motion to table may be renewed after progress. Instead of moving to reconsider a negative vote on the motion to table, just make another motion to table, since it is in order "after progress". And instead of moving to reconsider a positive vote on the motion to table, simply move to take from the table the motion that was tabled. In short, the motion to reconsider does not apply to the motion to table because there is no necessity for it.

Lesson XII

SUBSTITUTE MOTION AND AMENDMENT TO AN AMENDMENT

Two items are reserved for lesson XII because they are rather complicated. The first of these is an "amendment to an amendment". The principle involved is exactly the same as a primary amendment except that a primary amendment changes the original motion while a secondary amendment (amendment to an amendment) changes the primary amendment. Usually the change that can be made by an amendment to an amendment can also be made by a later primary amendment after the primary amendment now before the assembly has been disposed of.

The form for an amendment to an amendment (secondary amendment) is the same as for a primary amendment except that for the word "motion" you substitute the word "amendment". Thus if it is moved and seconded that we have a picnic and then it is moved and seconded that we amend the motion by adding the words "Friday afternoon", a proper secondary amendment would be to move that "we amend the amendment by striking out the word 'Friday' and inserting the word 'Saturday'." If seconded, the chairman would then state this amendment to the amendment as follows: "IT IS MOVED AND SECONDED THAT WE AMEND THE AMENDMENT BY STRIKING OUT THE WORD 'FRIDAY' AND INSERTING THE WORD 'SATURDAY', SO THAT THE AMENDMENT, IF AMENDED, WILL READ THAT WE AMEND THE MOTION BY ADDING THE WORDS 'SATURDAY AFTERNOON'. IS THERE ANY DISCUSSION ON THE AMENDMENT TO THE AMENDMENT?"

Put to VOTE:—"THE VOTE IS ON THE AMENDMENT TO THE AMENDMENT THAT WE (state the amendment to the amendment.) THOSE IN FAVOR OF THE AMENDMENT TO THE AMENDMENT SAY 'I'." (Pause) "THOSE OPPOSED TO THE AMENDMENT TO THE AMENDMENT SAY 'NO'."

'I' vote:—"THE 'I's' HAVE IT AND THE AMENDMENT TO THE AMENDMENT IS CARRIED. THE NEXT BUSINESS IS THE AMENDMENT *AS AMENDED* WHICH READS THAT WE (state amendment as amended.) IS THERE ANY DISCUSSION ON THE AMENDMENT *AS AMENDED*?" (Go next to manual, page 16 left, Put to *VOTE* phrase.)

'No' vote:—"THE 'NOES' HAVE IT AND THE AMENDMENT TO THE AMENDMENT IS LOST. IS THERE ANY DISCUSSION ON THE ORIGINAL AMENDMENT?" (Go next to manual, page 16 left, *Put to VOTE* phrase.)

The second item is a substitute motion. A substitute motion is really an amendment that differs from the ordinary amendment only in extent, that is, it substitutes an entirely new motion instead of changing just a part of the original motion. Because it is an entire motion it has the general status of another main motion and can be amended like a main motion and *should be amended* to suit the assembly before a vote is taken on making the substitution.

Also, because the original motion will be entirely removed if the substitution is made, the supporters of the original motion should be given opportunity to perfect the original motion by amendment before the vote is taken on making the substitution.

The procedure should be as follows:—

Member:—"MR. CHAIRMAN." (Pause for recognition.) "I MOVE, AS A SUBSTITUTE MOTION, THAT WE (state the substitute motion.")

Chairman:—"IT IS MOVED AND SECONDED AS A SUBSTITUTE MOTION THAT WE (state the substitute motion.) NOW THE CORRECT PROCEDURE IS FIRST TO PERFECT THE ORIGINAL MOTION BY AMENDMENTS, THEN PERFECT THE SUBSTITUTE MOTION BY AMENDMENTS, THEN VOTE ON MAKING THE SUBSTITUTION, AND FINALLY VOTE ON THE ADOPTION OF THE MOTION THEN BEFORE THE ASSEMBLY. IS THERE ANY DISCUSSION ON OR AMENDMENT TO THE ORIGINAL MOTION? — IF NOT, IS THERE ANY DISCUSSION ON OR AMENDMENT TO THE SUBSTITUTE MOTION? — IF NOT, THE VOTE IS ON SUBSTITUTING THIS LAST MOTION FOR THE ORIGINAL MOTION (as amended, if amended.) THOSE IN FAVOR OF MAKING THIS SUBSTITUTION SAY 'I'." (Pause) "THOSE OPPOSED TO MAKING THIS SUBSTITUTION SAY 'NO'."

'I' vote:—"THE 'I'S' HAVE IT AND THE NEW MOTION IS SUBSTITUTED FOR THE ORIGINAL MOTION. IS THERE ANY FURTHER DISCUSSION ON THE SUBSTITUTED MOTION?" (Go next to manual, page 18, *Put to VOTE* phrase.)

'No' vote:—"THE 'NOES' HAVE IT AND THE SUBSTITUTE MOTION IS LOST. IS THERE ANY FURTHER DISCUSSION ON THE ORIGINAL MOTION (or the motion as amended)?" (Go next to manual, page 18 left, *Put to VOTE* phrase.)

The usual but erroneous practice in making substitute motions is for the chairman to ask the mover of the original motion if he will accept the substitute motion in place of the original motion. If he does accept it, as does also the seconder of the original motion, then the chairman substitutes the new motion for the original one without a vote.

This procedure is improper because it disposes of the original motion without a majority vote of the assembly. That is to say, the mover of the original motion withdraws his original motion without asking for the unanimous consent of the assembly. (See page 9 in the manual as to procedure for *withdrawing* a motion.) (Also see lesson XV on Informal Procedure.)

Another common but erroneous practice is to vote on substituting the new motion for the original motion and then declare the substitute motion carried without further vote.

This is improper because it assumes that the assembly is in favor of adopting the substitute motion as it is without amendment when, as a matter of fact, the assembly voted only that they prefer the substitute motion to the original one. The assembly may very well prefer the substitute motion to the original one and still not be in favor of adopting either of them as they are.

AMENDMENT TO AMENDMENT AND SUBSTITUTE MOTION

It is time for "New Business".

Chairman:—"THE NEXT ON THE ORDER OF BUSINESS IS NEW BUSINESS. IS THERE ANY NEW BUSINESS?"

Mr. A:—"MR. CHAIRMAN."

Chairman:—"MR. A."

Mr. A:—"I MOVE THAT WE RENT A HALL FOR OUR CLUB MEETINGS."

Mr. B calls out, "I SECOND THE MOTION."

Chairman:—"IT IS MOVED AND SECONDED THAT WE RENT A HALL FOR OUR CLUB MEETINGS. IS THERE ANY DISCUSSION?"

Mr. C:—"MR. CHAIRMAN."

Chairman:—"MR. C."

Mr. C:—"WE HAVE CONSIDERABLE MONEY IN THE TREASURY AT PRESENT AND BUILDINGS ARE VERY CHEAP NOW. I THINK WE OUGHT TO BUY PERMANENT QUARTERS FOR THE CLUB WHILE

PRICES ARE SO LOW. THEREFORE, I MOVE THAT WE AMEND THIS MOTION BY STRIKING OUT THE WORD 'RENT' AND INSERTING THE WORD 'BUY'."

Mr. D calls out, "I SECOND THAT AMENDMENT."

Chairman:—"IT IS MOVED AND SECONDED THAT WE AMEND THE MOTION BY STRIKING OUT THE WORD 'RENT' AND INSERTING THE WORD 'BUY', SO THAT THE MOTION, IF AMENDED, WILL READ, THAT WE BUY A HALL FOR OUR CLUB MEETINGS. IS THERE ANY DISCUSSION ON THE AMENDMENT?"

Mr. E:—"MR. CHAIRMAN."

Chairman:—"MR. E."

Mr. E:—"BUYING A BUILDING IS A LARGE UNDERTAKING. WE SHOULD GO SLOWLY IN OBLIGATING THIS CLUB TO CARRY THROUGH SUCH A LARGE INVESTMENT. ALL THE CLUB MEMBERS SHOULD HAVE PLENTY OF TIME TO THINK IT OVER BEFORE WE TAKE THE FINAL STEP. THEREFORE, I MOVE THAT WE AMEND THE AMENDMENT BY ADDING THE WORDS 'AN OPTION ON' AFTER THE WORD 'BUY'."

Mr. F calls out, "I SECOND THE MOTION."

Chairman:—"IT IS MOVED AND SECONDED THAT WE AMEND THE AMENDMENT BY ADDING THE WORDS 'AN OPTION ON' AFTER THE WORD 'BUY' SO THAT THE AMENDMENT, IF AMENDED, WILL READ THAT WE AMEND THE MOTION BY STRIKING OUT THE WORD 'RENT' AND INSERTING THE WORDS 'BUY AN OPTION ON'. IS THERE ANY DISCUSSION ON THE AMENDMENT TO THE AMENDMENT?"

Mr. G:—"MR. CHAIRMAN."

Chairman:—"MR. G."

Mr. G:—"I THINK THERE SHOULD BE SOME LIMIT SET TO THE PRICE WE ARE TO PAY FOR A HALL. THEREFORE, I MOVE THAT WE AMEND THE MOTION BY ADDING THE WORDS 'TOTAL COST NOT TO EXCEED THREE THOUSAND DOLLARS'."

Chairman:—"YOUR AMENDMENT IS OUT OF ORDER BECAUSE THERE IS AN AMENDMENT PENDING AND ALSO AN AMENDMENT TO THAT AMENDMENT. IS THERE ANY FURTHER DISCUSSION ON THE AMENDMENT TO THE AMENDMENT?"

Mr. H:—"MR. CHAIRMAN."

Chairman:—"Mr. H."

Mr. H:—"I BELIEVE WE CAN SAVE TIME BY USING A SUBSTITUTE MOTION IN PLACE OF SO MANY DETAILED AMENDMENTS. THEREFORE, I MOVE AS A SUBSTITUTE MOTION THAT A BUILDING COMMITTEE OF THREE BE APPOINTED BY THE CHAIR TO SECURE AN OPTION ON THE PURCHASE OF A HALL FOR THIS CLUB, THE PRICE OF THE HALL NOT TO EXCEED THREE THOUSAND DOLLARS."

Mr. G:—"I SECOND THAT MOTION."

Chairman:—"IT IS MOVED AND SECONDED AS A SUBSTITUTE MOTION THAT A BUILDING COMMITTEE OF THREE BE APPOINTED BY THE CHAIR TO SECURE AN OPTION ON THE PURCHASE OF A HALL FOR THIS CLUB, THE PRICE OF THE HALL NOT TO EXCEED THREE THOUSAND DOLLARS. TO BE TECHNICALLY CORRECT WE SHOULD VOTE ON ALL AMENDMENTS BEFORE VOTING ON THE SUBSTITUTION. BUT THAT WOULD TAKE CONSIDERABLE TIME. IF THERE IS NO OBJECTION WE WILL VOTE ON THE SUBSTITUTION." (Pause. No objection.) "THEN THE VOTE IS ON THE SUBSTITUTION OF THIS LAST MOTION FOR THE ORIGINAL MOTION AND ITS PENDING AMENDMENTS. THOSE IN FAVOR OF THE SUBSTITUTION SAY 'I'." *(Pause. Many vote "I".)* "THOSE OPPOSED TO THE SUBSTITUTION SAY 'NO'." *(Only a few vote "No.") (The use of unanimous consent procedure to save time on points that have no opposition is explained and illustrated in lesson XV.)*

Chairman:—"THE 'I'S' HAVE IT AND THE LAST MOTION IS SUBSTITUTED FOR THE ORIGINAL MOTION AND ITS PENDING AMENDMENTS. IS THERE ANY DISCUSSION ON THE MOTION THAT A BUILDING COMMITTEE OF THREE BE APPOINTED BY THE CHAIR TO SECURE AN OPTION ON THE PURCHASE OF A HALL FOR THIS CLUB, THE PRICE OF THE HALL NOT TO EXCEED THREE THOUSAND DOLLARS?"

Many members call out, "QUESTION, QUESTION."

Chairman:—"IF THERE IS NO FURTHER DISCUSSION THE VOTE IS ON THE SUBSTITUTED MOTION THAT A BUILDING COMMITTEE OF THREE BE APPOINTED BY THE CHAIR TO SECURE AN OPTION ON THE PURCHASE OF A HALL FOR THIS CLUB,

THE PRICE OF THE HALL NOT TO EXCEED THREE THOUSAND DOLLARS. THOSE IN FAVOR OF THIS MOTION PLEASE STAND UP." *(20 stand up.)* "BE SEATED. THOSE OPPOSED PLEASE STAND UP." *(Three stand up.)* "Be SEATED."

Chairman:—"THE 'I'S' HAVE IT BY A VOTE OF 20 TO 3, AND THE MOTION TO APPOINT A BUILDING COMMITTEE IS CARRIED. I APPOINT MR. J. J. BROWN, MR. L. C. BLACK, AND MR. JOHN DAVIS AS THE MEMBERS OF THIS BUILDING COMMITTEE. IS THERE ANY OTHER BUSINESS?"

Note:—There are frequently several ways of handling particular situations. In the above case, this situation might have been handled by means of the motion to refer instead of by a substitute motion. The motion to refer would have been as follows:— "MR. CHAIRMAN." (Recognition.) "I MOVE THAT WE REFER THIS WHOLE QUESTION OF BUYING A HALL TO A BUILDING COMMITTEE OF THREE TO BE APPOINTED BY THE CHAIR, AND THAT THIS COMMITTEE BE INSTRUCTED TO INVESTIGATE AND REPORT ON AVAILABLE HALLS THAT WILL COST NOT TO EXCEED THREE THOUSAND DOLLARS."

A problem in procedure:—It has been moved, seconded and stated by the chair that we have a party in the gymnasium. It has been moved, seconded *and carried* that we amend this motion by adding the words "Friday night". Then a member of the club who just arrived at the meeting tells us that the gymnasium may be secured for the party on Saturday night but not on Friday night.

Explain how the time for the party may now be changed in accordance with the rules of parliamentary procedure, first by the use of the motion to reconsider and a secondary amendment, second, by the use of the motion to reconsider and a new primary amendment, third by the use of the motion to refer without changing the primary amendment already adopted.

Lesson XIII

APPEAL FROM THE DECISION OF THE CHAIR
OBJECTION TO CONSIDERATION

Appeals from the decision of the Chair are permitted in America (not in England; see Cushing's *Manual*) because appeals from the Chair to the assembly provide the only method of correcting an erroneous decision by the Chair and the only method of escaping from arbitrary and tyrannical rulings by the Chair.

However, appeals should be used sparingly because they are usually quite confusing to the average chairman and to the average assembly. The manual (page 6) gives the procedure to be used when an appeal is made.

In making any decision the Chair should state briefly, but immediately, the reason for his decision, such as, "The amendment to the main motion is out of order because the motion to refer is pending."

If the minority group uses appeals to delay action, the majority group should move to table every appeal that is debatable in order to keep the minority from wasting more time by debating the appeal. (See rule 5, page 6.)

If the assembly becomes arbitrary and, on an appeal, reverses the decision of the Chair when the Chair is obviously correct according to a clearly stated rule in the manual, the chairman should point out that this action is really amending the rules of procedure, rather than reversing the decision of the Chair. In such a case the Chair must decide whether to ignore this appeal and insist on the correct ruling or accept the appeal as a vote of lack of confidence in the chairman and resign forthwith.

This is, however, a delicate situation that should be handled in this drastic manner only when the rule of procedure involved is so obvious that there is no possibility of the Chair's being mistaken as to its interpretation. It is a poor chairman indeed who quits his post every time his feelings are hurt. He should resign his post only when the assembly has become so arbitrary in defying the established rules of procedure that the chairman is helpless because he no longer has any established rules to rely on in conducting the business of the organization.

The Chair is the agent of the majority chosen to conduct the business of the organization. A chairman should not be "touchy" about a temporary wave of feeling among the majority which results in a momentary action that is arbitrary, perhaps ridiculous. A chairman should be good enough sport to permit the assembly to have a little harmless fun at his expense occasionally. A sense of humor is, at times, quite as important as a sense of dignity. But a chairman should be quick to realize that he is of no service to the organization when the majority group has definitely lost confidence in him or become permanently hostile to him.

Objection to consideration is a motion that is seldom used, but is invaluable for a certain situation. When a member makes a motion that is obviously improper for the assembly to consider, or one that serves no purpose except to permit this member to say some nasty things about other members of the assembly, any other member may rise at once and "object to the consideration of this motion". This "objection to consideration" does not require a second, but it does require a two-thirds vote to sustain it.

Objection to consideration is a bit awkward for the Chair to handle because motions should never be put in negative form. In this case the Chair says, "Shall this question be considered? Those in favor of considering this question say 'I'." (*Pause.*) "Those opposed to considering this question say 'No'."

If the "Noes" have it by a two-thirds vote, then that question or motion is not considered. It is thrown out and cannot be re-introduced at that session. If, however, one more than one-third of the assembly vote in favor of consideration, then that question must be considered.

In this connection it should be noted that if one more than one-third of the assembly vote in favor of consideration, then the motion to table this main question is not immediately in order. (See rule 8, page 11R.) That is to say, when one more than one-third of the assembly vote for consideration, it is not permissable for the majority to cut off debate by means of the motion to table until after there has been some discussion on this original motion. (See Appendix to manual, page XXV.)

MANAGING AN ARBITRARY CHAIRMAN

Mr. Smith:—"MR. CHAIRMAN."

Chairman:—"MR. SMITH."

Mr. Smith:—"I MOVE THAT THE BUSINESS MEETING BE DISPENSED WITH THIS EVENING BECAUSE OF THE POOR VENTILATION IN THIS ROOM."

Another member calls out, "I SECOND THE MOTION."

Chairman:—"I RULE THAT MOTION OUT OF ORDER. YOU CAN PUT UP WITH THIS VENTILATION FOR THIRTY MINUTES."

Mr. Smith:—"MR. CHAIRMAN, I APPEAL FROM THE DE-CISION OF THE CHAIR."

Another member calls out, "I SECOND THE APPEAL."

Chairman:—"THERE IS AN APPEAL FROM THE DECISION OF THE CHAIR. IS THERE ANY DISCUSSION ON THIS APPEAL?"

Mr. Smith:—"MR. CHAIRMAN."

Chairman:—"MR. SMITH."

Mr. Smith:—"I BELIEVE IT IS THE PRIVILEGE OF THE ASSEMBLY TO DECIDE WHETHER WE ARE TO ENDURE THIS TERRIBLE VENTILATION FOR THIRTY MINUTES OR MORE."

Chairman:—"ARE YOU READY FOR THE QUESTION?"

Many call out, "QUESTION! QUESTION!"

Chairman:—"THOSE IN FAVOR OF SUSTAINING THE DECISION OF THE CHAIR SAY 'I'." *(A few vote "I".)* "THOSE OPPOSED TO SUSTAINING THE DECISION OF THE CHAIR SAY 'NO'." *(Many vote "No".)*

Chairman:—"THE 'NOES' HAVE IT AND THE DECISION OF THE CHAIR IS REVERSED BY VOTE OF THE ASSEMBLY. IS THERE ANY DISCUSSION ON THE MOTION TO DISPENSE WITH THE BUSINESS MEETING THIS EVENING?"

Chairman:—"IF NOT, THE VOTE IS ON THE MOTION TO DISPENSE WITH THE BUSINESS MEETING THIS EVENING. THOSE IN FAVOR SAY 'I'." *(Pause. Many vote "I".)* "THOSE OPPOSED SAY 'NO'." *(Only a few vote "No".)*

Chairman:—"THE 'I'S' HAVE IT, AND THE MOTION TO DISPENSE WITH THE BUSINESS MEETING IS CARRIED. THE NEXT THING IN ORDER IS THE ENTERTAINMENT. WILL THE CHAIRMAN OF THE ENTERTAINMENT COMMITTEE PLEASE TAKE CHARGE!"

MANAGING AN OBSTREPEROUS MEMBER

(At some point in the course of a business meeting) :—

Chairman:—"NEW BUSINESS IS NOW IN ORDER."

Mr. Red (the obstreperous member) :—"MR. CHAIRMAN."

Chairman:—"MR. RED."

Mr. Red:—"I MOVE THAT WE ENDORSE MR. JOHN BROWN AS CANDIDATE FOR MAYOR OF OUR CITY."

Mr. Green:—"I SECOND THE MOTION."

Chairman:—"IT IS CONTRARY TO THE POLICY OF THIS ORGANIZATION TO ENDORSE MEMBERS FOR POLITICAL OFFICE. HOWEVER, IF NO ONE OBJECTS I SHALL PUT THE QUESTION TO VOTE." *(Pause for objections.)*

Mr. Red:—"MR. CHAIRMAN, I BELIEVE THAT THE DIRTY CROOKS NOW IN OFFICE SHOULD BE—"

(Interruption.)

Mr. Smith:—"MR. CHAIRMAN, I OBJECT TO THE CONSIDERATION OF THIS QUESTION!"

Mr. Red:—"MR. CHAIRMAN, I RISE TO A POINT OF ORDER!"

Chairman:—"STATE YOUR POINT OF ORDER."

Mr. Red:—"I HAD THE FLOOR WHEN MR. SMITH INTERRUPTED. THEREFORE, HIS MOTION IS OUT OF ORDER."

Chairman:—"YOUR POINT IS NOT WELL TAKEN FOR TWO REASONS. FIRST, YOU DID NOT HAVE THE RIGHT TO THE FLOOR BECAUSE YOU BEGAN YOUR REMARKS WITHOUT BEING RECOGNIZED BY THE CHAIR. A SECOND REASON WHY YOUR POINT OF ORDER IS NOT WELL TAKEN IS BECAUSE OBJECTION TO CONSIDERATION MAY INTERRUPT A MEMBER WHO HAS THE FLOOR AND IS SPEAKING. MR. SMITH HAS MOVED OBJECTION TO CONSIDERATION. THOSE IN FAVOR OF CONSIDERING THE MOTION TO ENDORSE MR. JOHN BROWN FOR MAYOR SAY 'I'." *(Pause. Only a few vote "I".)* "THOSE OPPOSED TO CONSIDERING THIS MOTION SAY 'NO'." *(Almost all of the members vote "No".)*

Mr. Red:—"I CALL FOR A DIVISION."

Chairman: — "A DIVISION OF VOTE IS CALLED FOR. THOSE IN FAVOR OF CONSIDERING THE MOTION TO ENDORSE MR. JOHN BROWN FOR MAYOR, PLEASE STAND UP." *(Only Mr. Red and Mr. Green stand up.)* "BE SEATED. THOSE OPPOSED TO CONSIDERATION PLEASE STAND UP." *(Nearly all of the members stand up.)* "BE SEATED. THE 'NOES' HAVE IT BY A TWO-THIRDS VOTE AND THE MOTION TO ENDORSE MR. JOHN BROWN FOR MAYOR WILL NOT BE CONSIDERED. IS THERE ANY OTHER NEW BUSINESS?"

Mr. Red:—"MR. CHAIRMAN."

Chairman:—"MR. RED."

Mr. Red:—"I THINK IT IS A PITY THAT THIS ORGANIZATION WILL NOT ENDORSE ONE OF ITS OWN MEMBERS FOR MAYOR OF OUR CITY.—" (Interruption.)

Chairman:—"YOUR REMARKS ARE OUT OF ORDER, MR. RED. THE MEMBERS HAVE VOTED BY AN OVERWHELMING VOTE THAT WE WILL NOT CONSIDER THE ENDORSEMENT OF ANY CANDIDATE FOR POLITICAL OFFICE."

Mr. Red:—"I APPEAL FROM THE DECISION OF THE CHAIR."

Mr. Green:—"I SECOND THAT APPEAL."

Chairman:—"THERE IS AN APPEAL FROM THE DECISION OF THE CHAIR. I BELIEVE THIS KIND OF AN APPEAL IS NOT DEBATABLE.—" (Interruption.)

Mr. Smith:—"MR. CHAIRMAN."

Chairman:—"MR. SMITH."

Mr. Smith:—"WHETHER DEBATABLE OR NOT, I MOVE THAT THIS APPEAL BE LAID ON THE TABLE."

Another member calls out, "I SECOND THE MOTION TO TABLE."

Chairman:—"IT IS MOVED AND SECONDED THAT THIS APPEAL BE TABLED. THOSE IN FAVOR OF TABLING THIS APPEAL SAY 'I'." (Pause. Many vote "I".) "THOSE OPPOSED TO TABLING THIS APPEAL SAY 'NO'." (Only a few vote "No".)

Chairman:—"THE 'I'S' HAVE IT AND THE APPEAL IS TABLED. IS THERE ANY OTHER NEW BUSINESS?"

Lesson XIV

QUESTION OF PRIVILEGE AND PRIVILEGED QUESTIONS

Members of any organization have certain rights that are more important than any motion. These rights involve the comfort and convenience of the members, and the general welfare of the organization as a whole. If, for example, there is a bad draft of air from an open window causing members to sneeze and be otherwise uncomfortable, any member may rise at once, regardless of what business is being discussed, and ask, as a question of privilege, that the window be closed.

The procedure would be as follows:—(See manual, page 3.)

Member:—(Rising, but not waiting to be recognized) "MR. CHAIRMAN, I RISE TO A QUESTION OF PRIVILEGE!"

Chairman:—"STATE YOUR QUESTION OF PRIVILEGE."

Member:—"MAY WE HAVE THE WINDOW CLOSED?"

The Chair would then use his own judgment as to closing the window. Probably he would ask the sergeant at arms to close the window. If, in this case, someone objected to having the window closed, the Chair would have to have the assembly decide whether or not the window was to be closed. This motion to close the window, put to a vote by the Chair, would be a privileged motion because its nature is such as to demand immediate action.

The main business before the assembly when this question of privilege was raised would simply be suspended until this question of privilege and the resulting privileged motion were settled, then the pending business would be resumed just as though there had been no interruption.

Questions of privilege are taught this late in the course because they are quite annoying to a chairman and also because this kind of personal privilege is so frequently abused by thoughtless or antagonistic members.

The right to rise to a question of privilege is designed for extraordinary circumstances. Therefore, this right should not be used except under extraordinary circumstances. If a member rises to a question of privilege in order to annoy the chairman or to delay action, that member should be penalized by the Chair by being refused further recognition for any purpose until he has indicated his willingness to act in good faith thereafter.

It is one of the duties of the Chair to protect the assembly from the dilatory tactics and the show-off antics of any "procedurettes" present. A "procedurette" is a person who studies procedure in order to show off his knowledge of parliamentary law.

A few illustrations will demonstrate the highly involved nature of questions of privilege and of privileged questions raised as questions of privilege.

Chairman:—*(Sounds gavel)* "THE MEETING WILL PLEASE COME TO ORDER. IS THERE ANY NEW BUSINESS?"

Mr. A:—"MR. CHAIRMAN, I RISE TO A QUESTION OF PRIVILEGE!"

Chairman:—"STATE YOUR QUESTION OF PRIVILEGE."

Mr. A:—"THE OTHER MEMBERS OF THE AUDIT COMMITTEE ARE DOWNSTAIRS PLAYING CARDS BECAUSE THEY DID NOT EXPECT THIS MEETING TO BE CALLED TO ORDER BEFORE NINE O'CLOCK. I ASK PERMISSION TO NOTIFY THEM THAT THE MEETING HAS BEEN CALLED TO ORDER. THEY OUGHT TO BE HERE WHEN I MAKE THE AUDIT REPORT."

Chairman:—"PERMISSION IS GRANTED, PLEASE GET THEM HERE AS SOON AS POSSIBLE."

Mr. B:—"MR. CHAIRMAN, I RISE TO A POINT OF ORDER."

Chairman:—"STATE YOUR POINT OF ORDER."

Mr. B:—"I UNDERSTAND THAT THE AUDIT COMMITTEE IS TO REPORT AT THIS MEETING. DOESN'T A COMMITTEE REPORT TAKE PRECEDENCE OVER NEW BUSINESS?"

Chairman:—"YOUR POINT IS WELL TAKEN. THE AUDIT COMMITTEE REPORT IS THE MAIN ITEM FOR THIS MEETING, BUT I UNDERSTAND THAT THAT REPORT WILL TAKE MUCH TIME AND MAY CAUSE MUCH DISCUSSION. I CALLED FOR NEW BUSINESS FIRST SO AS TO GET EVERYTHING ELSE OUT OF THE WAY BEFORE CALLING ON THE AUDIT COMMITTEE FOR THEIR REPORT. IF THERE IS NO OBJECTION I SHALL AGAIN ASK FOR NEW BUSINESS. THE MEMBERS OF THE AUDIT COMMITTEE WILL BE HERE WITHIN A FEW MINUTES."

Mr. C (the treasurer):—"MR. CHAIRMAN."

Chairman:—"Mr. C."

Mr. C:—"I DESIRE TO RESIGN AS TREASURER OF THIS CLUB."

Chairman:—"YOUR RESIGNATION CANNOT BE CON-SIDERED, MR. C, UNTIL AFTER THE AUDIT COM-MITTEE HAS MADE ITS REPORT. YOU ARE A BONDED OFFICER AND YOU CANNOT BE RE-LIEVED OF THAT BOND UNTIL YOUR ACCOUNTS HAVE BEEN AUDITED."

Mr. C:—"I APPEAL FROM THE DICISION OF THE CHAIR."

Mr. D (a personal friend of Mr. C):—"I SECOND THAT AP-PEAL."

Chairman:—"THERE IS AN APPEAL FROM THE DECI-SION OF THE CHAIR. THE CHAIR HAS RULED THAT THE RESIGNATION OF THE TREASURER IS NOT IN ORDER UNTIL THE AUDIT COMMITTEE'S RE-PORT HAS BEEN ACCEPTED. THE AUDIT COMMIT-TEE WILL REPORT AT THIS MEETING, TONIGHT. AFTER THAT REPORT IS ACCEPTED THE RESIG-NATION OF THE TREASURER WILL BE IN ORDER IF HE SO DESIRES. THE CHAIR'S DECISION IS THAT THE TREASURER'S RESIGNATION IS NOT IN ORDER BEFORE THE REPORT OF THE AUDIT COM-MITTEE. THE QUESTION IS, SHALL THE DECISION OF THE CHAIR BE SUSTAINED. THOSE IN FAVOR OF SUSTAINING THE DECISION OF THE CHAIR SAY 'I'." (Many vote "I".) "THOSE OPPOSED TO SUS-TAINING THE DECISION OF THE CHAIR SAY 'NO'." (A few vote "No".)

Chairman:—"THE 'I'S' SEEM TO HAVE IT." (Pause) "THE 'I'S' HAVE IT AND THE DECISION OF THE CHAIR IS SUSTAINED. THE RESIGNATION OF THE TREAS-URER IS NOT IN ORDER AT THIS TIME. I SEE THAT THE MEMBERS OF THE AUDIT COMMITTEE ARE HERE NOW. WILL THE CHAIRMAN OF THE AUDIT COMMITTEE PLEASE READ THE REPORT OF THAT COMMITTEE!"

Mr. A (chairman of the Audit Committee):—"MR. CHAIR-MAN, I RISE TO A QUESTION OF PRIVILEGE."

Chairman:—"STATE YOUR QUESTION OF PRIVILEGE."

Mr. A:—"THIS AUDIT REPORT INVOLVES CONSIDER-ABLE CRITICISM OF CERTAIN ACTS OF THIS CLUB AND OF CERTAIN MEMBERS OF THE CLUB. THERE-FORE, AS A QUESTION OF PRIVILEGE, I MOVE THAT ALL GUESTS AND MEMBERS NOT IN GOOD STANDING BE ASKED TO LEAVE THE ROOM UN-TIL THIS REPORT IS READ AND THEN ACCEPTED, REJECTED, OR OTHERWISE DISPOSED OF BY THE CLUB."

Mr. K:—"I SECOND THE MOTION."

Chairman:—"YOUR PRIVILEGE IS GRANTED. AS A QUESTION OF PRIVILEGE IT IS MOVED AND SECONDED THAT ALL GUESTS AND MEMBERS NOT IN GOOD STANDING BE ASKED TO LEAVE THE ROOM DURING THE READING AND CONSIDERATION OF THE REPORT OF THE AUDIT COMMITTEE. IS THERE ANY DISCUSSION ON THIS PRIVILEGED MOTION?"

Mr. J:—"MR. CHAIRMAN."

Chairman:—"MR. J."

Mr. J:—"IT SEEMS TO ME THAT WE ARE WASTING A LOT OF TIME IN GETTING TO THIS REPORT OF THE AUDIT COMMITTEE. FURTHERMORE, IT IS QUITE A DISCOURTESY TO ASK OUR GUESTS TO LEAVE THE ROOM ALMOST AS SOON AS THEY GET HERE. SINCE THE REPORT OF THE AUDIT COMMITTEE IS IN ORDER NOW, WHY DON'T THEY REPORT?"

Chairman:—"THE REPORT OF THE AUDIT COMMITTEE WILL NOT BE IN ORDER UNTIL THIS PRIVILEGED QUESTION IS DECIDED. THE CHAIRMAN OF THE AUDIT COMMITTEE WAS QUITE WITHIN HIS RIGHTS TO MAKE THIS PRIVILEGED MOTION. AS A MATTER OF FACT IT WAS HIS DUTY AS CHAIRMAN OF YOUR AUDIT COMMITTEE TO RAISE THIS QUESTION OF PRIVILEGE AND MAKE THIS MOTION IF HE THINKS THIS AUDIT REPORT IS OF SUCH A NATURE THAT IT SHOULD BE READ ONLY TO MEMBERS OF THIS CLUB IN GOOD STANDING. ARE YOU READY TO VOTE ON THIS PRIVILEGED MOTION?"

A number of members call out, "QUESTION! QUESTION! QUESTION!"

Chairman:—"THE VOTE IS ON THE MOTION THAT GUESTS AND MEMBERS NOT IN GOOD STANDING BE ASKED TO LEAVE THE ROOM DURING THE READING AND CONSIDERATION OF THE AUDIT COMMITTEE REPORT. THOSE IN FAVOR SAY 'I'." *(Quite a few vote "I.")*

"THOSE OPPOSED SAY 'NO'." *(Quite a few vote "No".)*

Chairman:—"THE CHAIR IS IN DOUBT. THOSE IN FAVOR OF THE MOTION TO ASK THE GUESTS TO LEAVE THE ROOM PLEASE RAISE THE RIGHT HAND." *(23 raise their hand.)* "THOSE OPPOSED PLEASE RAISE THE RIGHT HAND." *(18 raise their hand.)*

Chairman:—"THE 'I'S' HAVE IT AND THE PRIVILEGED MOTION IS CARRIED. WILL THE GUESTS AND MEMBERS NOT IN GOOD STANDING PLEASE LEAVE THE ROOM!" *(Pause while they leave the room.)*

After the guests have left the room the Chair continues:—

Chairman:—"WILL THE CHAIRMAN OF THE AUDIT COMMITTEE PLEASE READ HIS REPORT!"

Mr. C (the treasurer):—"MR. CHAIRMAN, I RISE TO A QUESTION OF PRIVILEGE."

Chairman:—"STATE YOUR QUESTION OF PRIVILEGE."

Mr. C:—"I DO NOT NEED TO HEAR THIS REPORT BECAUSE I HAVE READ IT ALREADY. THEREFORE, I ASK PERMISSION TO LEAVE THE ROOM ALONG WITH THE OTHER MEMBERS NOT IN GOOD STANDING."

Chairman:—"YOUR PRIVILEGE IS NOT GRANTED, MR. C, BECAUSE YOU SHOULD BE HERE TO ANSWER ANY QUESTIONS THAT MAY BE ASKED BY THE MEMBERS AS TO THE OPERATION OF THE TREASURER'S OFFICE DURING THE LAST YEAR."

Mr. C:—"I APPEAL FROM THE DECISION OF THE CHAIR. I DO NOT SEE WHY I SHOULD LISTEN TO THAT TIRESOME REPORT A SECOND TIME."

Mr. D:—"I SECOND THAT APPEAL."

Chairman:—"THERE IS AN APPEAL FROM THE DECISION OF THE CHAIR. THE DECISION OF THE CHAIR IS THAT THE TREASURER, MR. C, SHOULD NOT BE GIVEN PERMISSION TO LEAVE THE ROOM AT THIS TIME BECAUSE HE OUGHT TO BE HERE TO ANSWER QUESTIONS THAT MAY BE ASKED BY MEMBERS CONCERNING THE AUDIT REPORT OR THE WORK OF THE TREASURER'S OFFICE DURING THIS LAST YEAR. THOSE IN FAVOR OF SUSTAINING THE DECISION OF THE CHAIR PLEASE RAISE THE RIGHT HAND." *(20 raise their hand.)* "THOSE OPPOSED TO SUSTAINING THE DECISION OF THE CHAIR PLEASE RAISE THE RIGHT HAND." *(A few raise their hand, many not voting.)*

Chairman:—"THE DECISION OF THE CHAIR IS SUSTAINED BY VOTE OF THE MEMBERS. WILL THE CHAIRMAN OF THE AUDIT COMMITTEE PLEASE READ THE REPORT OF HIS COMMITTEE!"

Mr. A (chairman of Audit Committee):—"MR. CHAIRMAN."

Chairman:—"MR. A."

Mr. A:—"THE AUDIT COMMITTEE HAS GONE OVER THE BOOKS, VOUCHERS, AND OTHER RECORDS OF THE TREASURER'S OFFICE FOR THE LAST YEAR AND HAS INSTRUCTED ME TO READ THE FOLLOWING REPORT." *(He then reads the report.)*

Footnote:—This report of the audit committee should be accepted, rejected, or referred back to the audit committee for further consideration. In case the assembly thinks that this particular audit committee is unfair or unreasonable in their report, the assembly should discharge this audit committee, have a new committee appointed, and then refer this first audit committee report to the new audit committee for further investigation and consideration.

Lesson XV

INFORMAL PROCEDURE
UNANIMOUS CONSENT — COURTESY VOTES

It is a mistake for a chairman to be unnecessarily formal. Matters of importance should, of course, be decided by a formal vote. But when there is obviously general approval on minor details these details should be handled informally by unanimous consent.

For example—

Mr. A:—"MR. CHAIRMAN."

Chairman:—"MR. A."

Mr. A:—"I MOVE THAT WE HAVE A SUPPER DANCE NEXT FRIDAY NIGHT."

Mr. B:—"I SECOND THE MOTION."

Chairman:—"IT IS MOVED AND SECONDED THAT WE HAVE A SUPPER DANCE NEXT FRIDAY NIGHT. IS THERE ANY DISCUSSION?"

Mr. C:—"MR. CHAIRMAN."

Chairman:—"MR. C."

Mr. C:—"I AM ENTIRELY IN FAVOR OF THE PROPOSED DANCE. BUT I SUGGEST THAT THE WORD 'SUPPER' BE CHANGED TO THE WORD 'DINNER' BECAUSE IT IS CUSTOMARY TO CALL SUCH AN AFFAIR A 'DINNER DANCE' REGARDLESS OF HOW LATE THE DINNER MAY BE SCHEDULED."

Chairman:—"I BELIEVE YOU ARE CORRECT. DO YOU ACCEPT THAT CHANGE MR. A?"

Mr. A:—"YES. I ACCEPT THAT CHANGE."

Chairman:—"THEN IF THERE IS NO OBJECTION THE WORD 'SUPPER' WILL BE CHANGED TO 'DINNER'. IS THERE FURTHER DISCUSSION ON THE MOTION TO HAVE A DINNER DANCE NEXT FRIDAY NIGHT?"

Mr. D:—"MR. CHAIRMAN, I RISE TO A QUESTION OF PRIVILEGE?"

Chairman:—"STATE YOUR QUESTION OF PRIVILEGE."

Mr. D:—"IT IS VERY WARM IN THIS ROOM. MAY WE HAVE THE WINDOWS OPENED A LITTLE?"

Chairman:—"IF THERE IS NO OBJECTION, THE SER-
GEANT AT ARMS WILL OPEN THE WINDOWS FOR
VENTILATION."

(Note. If some one does object then a formal vote is necessary
to determine whether the windows are, or are not, to be opened.
In very cold weather the persons near the windows may be just
as insistent on keeping the windows closed as others are on having them opened.)

Chairman:—(Continuing after windows are opened) "IS THERE
FURTHER DISCUSSION ON THE MOTION TO HAVE
A DINNER DANCE?" (Pause.) "IF NOT, THE VOTE IS
ON THE MOTION TO HAVE A DINNER DANCE.
THOSE IN FAVOR SAY 'I'." (Pause.) "THOSE OP-
POSED SAY 'NO'."

A Courtesy Vote

There is one situation in which the negative vote is not called
for; that is where the vote is merely an act of courtesy. For instance, when a guest speaker has given an address it is common
practice for some member to move that the speaker be given a
rising vote of thanks.

The chairman says, "IT IS MOVED AND SECONDED
THAT WE GIVE OUR GUEST SPEAKER A RISING VOTE
OF THANKS. THOSE IN FAVOR PLEASE RISE." (Pause.
The members rise and frequently applaud also.)

In this case the negative vote is not called for because, after
all, nothing is being decided that binds the organization in any
way. Nevertheless, a few negative votes would be quite a discourtesy to the guest speaker and would embarass him considerably.

However, both the chairman and the members should see to
it that these courtesy votes are not used as an endorsement of
the cause which the speaker presented in his speech or as an endorsement of the speaker personally for some office for which
he is a candidate.

Nothing short of intelligence, watchfulness, and loyalty to
the group will suffice to keep a given group from being used by
ambitious persons to further their own selfish ends. An intelligent, alert chairman can easily prevent any member from thus
violating the rules and purposes of the organization by refusing
to put an improper motion to a vote or by calling the attention of
the group to the danger involved in the motion presented to them
for a vote.

But when the chairman is disloyal to the aims and purposes
of the group, it is not so easy for loyal members to keep improper
motions from coming before the assembly for consideration and
vote. Therefore, when a chairman persists in attempts to divert

the group from its established rules and purposes, it is both proper and wise for the loyal members to move "that the chairman be censored for ignoring the rules and purposes of the organization".

Of course, the quickest way to deal with an improper motion moved by any member and stated by the Chair, is to "rise to a point of order" and then state that the motion before the assembly is improper because it violates the rules or purposes of the group. And if the Chair decides that "your point is not well taken", you can appeal from the Chair's decision to the assembly. *(See appeals, page 6 in manual. Also see lesson XIII.)*

If two-thirds of the group are opposed to the consideration of the motion in question it can be "thrown out" just as soon as it is moved by the use of "objection to consideration". *(See page 11 in the manual. Also see lesson XIII.)*

Lesson XVI

NOMINATIONS AND ELECTIONS

NOMINATIONS

One outstanding duty of the citizen is to help choose the leaders of his group. This is done by means of nominations and elections. In small groups nominations are usually made "from the floor", that is, a member rises and addresses the Chair. When recognized by the Chair the member says, "I nominate Mr. John H. Smith for president". A nomination by this method does not require a second, but other members may desire to "second" this nomination just to show that they support Mr. J. H. Smith for this office. When there are no other nominations to be made some member should move, "that nominations close". If this motion is seconded and adopted by a two thirds vote, nominations are closed and the group may then proceed with the final election.

Another form of nomination is to have a nominating committee make up a list of one or more nominees for each elective office and present these nominations to the group in the form of a committee report. Frequently this form of nomination is supplemented by "nominations from the floor". A nominating committee has the advantage that it can consult each nominee in advance and be sure that the nominee will accept the nomination when it is made. Also, a nominating committee can make up "a slate" of nominees for the various offices who will work together harmoniously if all the members of this "slate" are elected. It is a misfortune for any group to have a chairman and a secretary who do not cooperate cordially in conducting the affairs of the group.

A third method of nomination for an elective office is to have a certain number of members (one or more) sign a petition placing Mr. J. H. Smith in nomination for the office of president. This method is too slow and cumbersome except for a very large group.

A PRACTICE NOMINATION

Chairman: "THE MEETING WILL COME TO ORDER. THE FIRST ITEM OF BUSINESS TODAY IS THE NOMINATION OF CANDIDATES FOR THE ANNUAL ELECTION TO BE HELD AT THE NEXT REGULAR MEETING. ALL NOMINATIONS ARE TO BE MADE FROM THE FLOOR. NOMINATIONS FOR THE OFFICE OF PRESIDENT ARE NOW IN ORDER."

Mr. A:—"MR. CHAIRMAN."

Chairman:—"MR. A."

Mr. A :—"I NOMINATE JOHN BLACK."

Chairman :—"JOHN BLACK IS NOMINATED."

Mr. B :—"MR. CHAIRMAN."

Chairman :—"MR. B."

Mr. B :—"I NOMINATE MARY BROWN."

Chairman :—"MARY BROWN IS NOMINATED."

Miss C :—"MR. CHAIRMAN."

Chairman :—"MISS C."

Miss C :—"I SECOND THE NOMINATION OF MARY BROWN."

Mr. D :—"MR. CHAIRMAN."

Chairman :—"MR. D."

Mr. D :—"I SECOND THE NOMINATION OF MARY BROWN."

Chairman :—"ARE THERE FURTHER NOMINATIONS?"

Miss E :—"MR. CHAIRMAN."

Chairman :—"MISS E."

Miss E :—"I NOMINATE WALTER JONES."

Chairman :—"WALTER JONES IS NOMINATED."

Miss C :—"MR. CHAIRMAN."

Chairman :—"MISS C."

Miss C :—"I NOMINATE CHARLES BRADFORD."

Chairman :—"MISS C HAS ALREADY SECONDED THE NOMINATION OF ONE CANDIDATE AND THEREFORE CANNOT NOMINATE ANOTHER CANDIDATE. IN SOME STATES THERE IS A LAW AGAINST SIGNING THE PETITION OF MORE THAN ONE CANDIDATE FOR THE SAME OFFICE."

Mr. F :—"MR. CHAIRMAN."

Chairman :—"MR. F."

Mr. F :—"I NOMINATE CHARLES BRADFORD."

Chairman :—"CHARLES BRADFORD IS NOMINATED."

Mr. A :—"MR. CHAIRMAN."

Chairman :—"MR. A."

Mr. A:—"I MOVE THAT NOMINATIONS CLOSE."

Mr. F:—*(without waiting for recognition)* "I SECOND THAT MOTION."

Chairman:—*(momentarily ignoring that motion)* "ARE THERE OTHER NOMINATIONS?" *(After a pause in which no further nominations are made.)* "IF NOT, IT IS MOVED AND SECONDED THAT NOMINATIONS CLOSE. THOSE IN FAVOR OF CLOSING NOMINATIONS SAY 'I'." *(Pause)* "THOSE OPPOSED SAY 'NO'."

Chairman:—"THE 'I's' HAVE IT BY A TWO-THIRDS VOTE AND THE MOTION TO CLOSE NOMINATIONS FOR THE OFFICE OF PRESIDENT IS CARRIED. NOMINATIONS ARE NOW IN ORDER FOR THE OFFICE OF VICE-PRESIDENT."

Note: Nominations may be reopened by a simple majority vote when there is occasion for doing so.

NOMINATION BY NOMINATING COMMITTEE

Chairman:"THE MEETING WILL COME TO ORDER. THE FIRST ITEM OF BUSINESS TODAY IS THE REPORT OF THE NOMINATING COMMITTEE. AT THE LAST MEETING MOLLIE BLACK, CHESTER BRADLEY, AND FRANK OAKLEY WERE SELECTED AS THE NOMINATING COMMITTEE. IS THE NOMINATING COMMITTEE READY TO REPORT?"

Mollie Black:—"MR. CHAIRMAN."

Chairman:—"MISS BLACK."

Mollie Black:—"IN ACCORDANCE WITH THE PROVISIONS OF THE CONSTITUTION YOUR NOMINATING COMMITTEE DESIRES TO PLACE IN NOMINATION THE FOLLOWING PERSONS:
FOR PRESIDENT, MARY BROWN; FOR VICE-PRESIDENT, CHESTER WINSLOW; FOR SECRETARY, VIRGINIA BRADFORD; FOR TREASURER, FRANK LUDLOW; FOR SERGEANT AT ARMS, FRED BRITTON."

Chairman:—"YOU HAVE HEARD THE REPORT OF THE NOMINATING COMMITTEE. OUR CONSTITUTION ALSO PROVIDES FOR NOMINATIONS FROM THE FLOOR. ARE THERE OTHER NOMINATIONS FOR PRESIDENT? *(Pause. Hearing no nominations, he continues)* FOR VICE-PRESIDENT? *(Pause, hearing none)* FOR SECRETARY? *(Pause, hearing none)* FOR TREASURER? *(Pause, hearing none)* FOR SERGEANT AT ARMS?"

Chairman:—"IF THERE ARE NO OTHER NOMINATIONS WILL SOMEONE PLEASE MOVE THAT NOMINATIONS CLOSE AND THAT THE SECRETARY BE INSTRUCTED TO CAST A BALLOT FOR THE 'SLATE' OF NOMINEES PRESENTED BY THE NOMINATING COMMITTEE."

Note:—This suggestion by the chairman that someone move that the secretary be instructed to cast a ballot for the nominees would be out of order at this meeting if the Constitution provided that nominations be made at one meeting and the election be held at the next meeting. Even a unanimous vote can not suspend the Constitution unless the Constitution specifically provides for such suspension (which it usually does not).

Chester Bradley:—"I MOVE THAT NOMINATIONS CLOSE AND THAT THE SECRETARY BE INSTRUCTED TO CAST A BALLOT FOR THE 'SLATE' OF NOMINEES."

Frank Oakley:—*(without waiting to be recognized)* "I SECOND THE MOTION."

Chairman:—"IT IS MOVED AND SECONDED THAT NOMINATIONS CLOSE AND THAT THE SECRETARY BE INSTRUCTED TO CAST A BALLOT FOR THE 'SLATE' OF NOMINEES PRESENTED BY OUR NOMINATING COMMITTEE. THOSE IN FAVOR OF THIS MOTION SAY 'I'." *(Pause. Many vote "I".)* "THOSE OPPOSED SAY 'NO'." *(None vote "No".)*

Chairman:—"THE 'I's' HAVE IT UNANIMOUSLY AND THE MOTION IS CARRIED. THE SECRETARY WILL CAST A BALLOT FOR EACH OF THE NOMINEES. IS THERE ANY OTHER BUSINESS?"

Note:—In case someone votes "No" on the above motion, the motion is lost because it requires a unanimous vote. When this motion is lost because of one or more negative votes, the chairman may ask those voting in the negative to make other nominations since they seem to be opposed to the present nominees. But whether other nominations are made or not, a separate vote must be taken for each office to be filled when the motion "to instruct the secretary to cast a ballot" has been defeated by one or more negative votes.

As a matter of fact, formal nominations are not necessary for an election. The members may proceed to "ballot" on the election of a "president" for instance, and each member may write on his ballot the name of the person he desires for president. Then the ballots are counted and all the names written on the ballots are listed as candidates with the number of ballots received by each candidate listed after the name of that candidate. If only a plurality vote is required for election the candidate with the largest vote on the first ballot is declared elected. If a majority vote is required for election then some rule must be followed for the succeeding balloting that will insure a majority vote for some one candidate after a reasonable number of votes have been taken. The usual rule in such cases is to drop the candidate with the smallest vote after each balloting until a majority vote is secured. Sometimes the rule is adopted that after the first ballot all but the two candidates with the highest votes are dropped. This simple rule guarantees a majority vote at the end of two ballotings. However, this system offers clever politicians an easy opportunity to eliminate good candidates on the first ballot by nominating other candidates who will "split-the-vote" of the good candidates so that the two candidates who survive the first ballot may not be the two strongest candidates in the list of original nominees.

Note:—The best method of preventing this political trickery is by using the single-transferable-vote system described in the section below on Elections.

ELECTIONS

When the candidates for an elective office have been nominated, the next step is to elect one of the nominees for the office to be filled. For this purpose two general systems are used, majority election and plurality election. In a plurality election the candidate having the largest number of votes is declared elected even though this candidate actually received only twenty-five per cent of the total vote. In fact, if there are ten nominees one of them may be elected under this system by a vote of twelve per cent if each of the other nine candidates receives close to ten per cent of the total vote.

However, the majority vote system is considered the better system because it guarantees that the leader elected represents the choice of a majority of the members. There is no system of choosing leaders that will *guarantee* successful leadership, but obviously a leader with a majority supporting him at the beginning of his term of office has a better chance to be a real leader of the group than a leader with the support of only twenty per cent of the membership at the beginning of his term of office.

There are two systems of choosing officers by majority vote: one is the system of double elections, that is, a primary election to reduce the number of candidates to two, and a final election to choose between these two. This is the system in most common use in the United States. The other system is called the "single-transferable-vote system" because you mark your first, second, third and perhaps a fourth choice on the ballot and then your second choice vote is counted if your first choice candidate runs lowest in the count of the first choice votes. This system does away with two elections but it does take a little more time to count the ballots.

Under this single-transferable-vote system all the first choice votes are counted and placed in piles, one pile for each candidate. Then, if no candidate gets a majority of the total vote, the candidate having the smallest first choice vote is declared "out of the race" and his first choice ballots are all recounted in accordance with the second choice indicated on each ballot. If the addition of these second choice ballots does not give any candidate a majority of the total vote, the candidate with the lowest total on this second count is declared out of the race and his ballots are re-counted according to the next choice on each ballot. This system of dropping off the lowest candidate continues either until one candidate does get a majority of the total vote, or, failing in that, until there is only one candidate remaining. Usually, one candidate will eventually secure a majority under this system if the voters will indicate their second, third and fourth choices as well as their first choice. Voters should mark a second, third and fourth choice under this system, because the second choice is not a vote against the first choice owing to the fact that the second choice is not counted until the first choice is declared "out of the race."

In principle this single-transferable-vote system is the same as the double election system because in a primary election you vote your first choice and then, when your first choice candidate is eliminated in the primary, you go to the voting booth at the final election and vote your second choice. Under the single-transferable-vote system you indicate both your first and second choice at the one election so that when your first choice candidate turns out to be the "tail end" candidate, the election officials can go ahead and count your vote for your second choice because you have already indicated your second choice on the one and only ballot.

No illustration is necessary to explain the ordinary primary and secondary (or final) election. One ballot is taken and if no one gets a majority of all the votes cast, all but the two leading candidates are dropped from the contest and then a second vote is taken on the two remaining candidates.

The other majority vote system (the single-transferable-vote system) requires some illustration to make it clear. The voter indicates his first, second, third and fourth choice by the numbers 1, 2, 3 and 4. The voter marking the ballot to the right voted for Mary Brown as his 1st choice, Walter Jones as his second choice and John Black as his third choice.

Ballot	Choice
John Black	3
Mary Brown	1
Walter Jones	2
Charles Bradford	

He refused to give Charles Bradford his fourth choice because
he did not want Charles Bradford as president under any cir-
cumstance.

When the ballots for this class of thirty members were counted according to the first choice votes the count was as indicated
in the first count column below.

	1st Count 1st Choice only	Jones' Ballots 2nd Choice	2nd Count 1st & 2nd Choice	Bradford's Ballots 2nd Choice	3rd Count
Candidate					
John Black	8	1	9	2	11
Mary Brown	10	3	13	5	18
Walter Jones	4	—	—	—	—
Charles Bradford	8	0	8	—	—
Wasted Ballots	—	—	—	1	1
Total Ballots	30	4	30	8	30

The first choice ballots are arranged in piles by the "tellers"
with all of the eight John Black 1st choice ballots in one pile, all
of the ten Mary Brown 1st choice ballots in another pile, etc.

Since no candidate has a majority of all the votes cast the
candidate with the smallest vote, Walter Jones, is declared "out
of the race" and his four 1st choice ballots are re-distributed according to their 2nd choice indication. (See 2nd column above.)
Adding these 1st and 2nd choices together gives the second count
which is 9, 13 and 8 respectively for the three remaining candidates. Still no candidate has a majority of all the votes cast,
consequently, the candidate with the smallest vote in this 2nd
count, Charles Bradford, must be dropped and his eight 1st choice
ballots re-distributed according to their 2nd choice indication
which is shown in column 4. One of the Charles Bradford 1st
choice ballots had no 2nd choice indicated, therefore it was a
"wasted ballot" when Bradford was declared "out of the race."
These second choice ballots for John Black and Mary Brown are
added to their previous total of 9 and 13 respectively to make
the 3rd count of 11 for John Black and 18 for Mary Brown. Mary
Brown now has 18 ballots which is 2 more than a majority of the
total vote cast, therefore, Mary Brown is declared elected to the
office of president for the next year.

By this system a group can select its officers by majority
vote with one brief election no matter how many candidates are
nominated. The counting of the ballots may take some time, but
this need not delay the group as a whole. Three "tellers" can
take the ballots to another room and do the counting (if desirable,
under the supervision of the candidates or their representatives)

while the group as a whole adjourns, or proceeds to take up other business.

Committees are usually appointed by the Chair. But where it is preferred that the members of a committee be elected, several methods of election are available. If it is a committee of five, each member may vote for any five candidates and the five candidates with the largest vote are declared elected. (This is called straight election-at-large.) This method has the disadvantage that a bare majority of fifty-five per cent of the members may elect all the members of this committee, leaving the forty-five per cent minority of the club membership without any representation on this important committee.

A simple system that guarantees some representation for a strong minority is that known as limited voting. If a committee of five is to be elected, each voter is allowed only one vote (instead of five as above). Under this system it will usually work out that the fifty-five per cent majority will elect three members of the committee while the forty-five per cent minority will elect two members.

The most accurate system of choosing a committee or a board of directors that accurately represents each group in the club in proportion to its numerical strength is known as the "Hare System of Proportional Representation," but this system is too complicated to be explained here. (See description of this system in the Encyclopedia Brittanica.) The ballot is the same as that used to elect a president by the single-transferable-vote system described above, but the counting of the ballots is much more complicated.

When there is a tie vote for two candidates, the tie is usually broken by flipping a coin. Since half the group favor the one candidate, it does not matter much which one is finally chosen, consequently, deciding it by chance is the simplest solution of the problem.

Lesson XVII

SECRETARY AND MINUTES

The secretary (or clerk) of an organization is the next officer in importance to the chairman because he (or she) keeps the official record of the action of the organization. However, there are many organizations in which the secretary is the officer of most importance. This is when the secretary is the one who knows all the past history and precedents of the organization and tells the chairman just how things have been done in the past and should be done in the future. In these instances the chairman may change every year, but the secretary is re-elected (or re-hired) year after year.

In addition to keeping accurate minutes of each meeting, the secretary must have a thorough knowledge of parliamentary procedure, must be able to read papers and communications to the assembly with a clear voice, and must be able to preside in the absence of the chairman and vice-chairman.

Since the secretaryship is primarily a working job rather than an honorary one, the secretary should be chosen because of his (or her) accuracy, speed in taking notes, and knowledge of procedure rather than because of popularity. The business of the organization is soon in chaos if the secretary is unable to present the old business and the new business in proper order or fails to keep accurate minutes of the various meetings.

The final report of the minutes, sometimes called "The Journal," should be typed or written legibly in ink, never in pencil. The minutes should tell the kind of meeting (regular or special) the date of the meeting, the name of the organization and the name of the presiding officer. The minutes should contain a record of all the formal actions of the organization and this should be certified by the signature of the secretary. When these minutes are approved at the next meeting this action should be recorded at the bottom of the minutes as follows:—

"Approved as read (or approved as corrected) May 26, 1932.

Signature of Secretary.

Since the secretary should not slow up the business of the meeting by taking time to write out every action in full, some rapid system of note-taking should be used. The following is offered as one good system of note-taking.

MATERIALS FOR NOTE-TAKING

The secretary should have on hand a good pen and plenty of ink, or not less than two pencils well sharpened. For paper, a loose-leaf notebook is best if the pages are securely fastened. Loose sheets of paper may be blown from the table by an unexpected gust of wind, making it necessary to delay the business of the meeting while the secretary collects the scattered papers from the floor.

The minutes of the previous meeting should be immediately to the left, (in front) of the blank pages to be used for recording the business of the current meeting. This makes it easy to refer to the past action of the organization when there is occasion for doing so.

To facilitate the business of a meeting the secretary should make a list of the old business at the top of the blank page to be used in recording the notes of this meeting. For example:—

OLD BUSINESS FOR MEETING OF NOV. 2, 1932.
    To have a picnic—Tabled Oct. 26.
    To have a dance—Postponed (Oct. 26) to Nov. 2.
    To raise dues—Referred to Finance Com. for report at Nov. 2 meeting.
    To buy a radio—Pending at adjournment. (Unfinished Business.)

"Old business" includes motions referred to committees, motions postponed to later meetings and motions tabled, as well as "unfinished business" which is the motion (if any) that was pending when the last meeting was adjourned. The motions referred to committee may come back before the assembly as committee reports. The motions postponed till a later meeting come before the assembly again as general orders or special orders. The motions laid on the table may be brought before the assembly again by the motion "to take from the table." (See bottom of page 12 in manual.) The motion that was pending at the time of adjournment of the last meeting (and is, therefore, unfinished business) comes up automatically at the next meeting at the time specified in the "Order of Business" for unfinished business.

GENERAL AND SPECIAL ORDERS

An "order" is something which a majority (perhaps an extraordinary majority) of the assembly has commanded. If a majority of the assembly orders that the motion to have a radio be considered at the November second meeting, then this motion to have a radio has precedence at the November second meeting over a motion that is sponsored by only two members of the assembly such as a new motion to have a Christmas Party.

Obviously the majority of the assembly should have the authority, when they desire it, to say what motions are to be considered at the next meeting and in what order. The command (by the motion to postpone) that a certain matter be considered at the next meeting is called a "general order." The command that a certain matter be considered at a certain definite time ("at 3 o'clock" or "immediately after the reading of the minutes") is called a "special order." To create a special order requires a two-thirds vote. (See pages 8 and 14 in manual.) And a special order can not be changed except by a two-thirds vote. Usually general and special orders are created by means of the motion "to postpone to a certain day" (see page 14 in manual). However, these orders may be created by a main motion. For example, when there is no other business before the assembly a member may rise and say, "Mr. Chairman." The chairman recognizes him:—"Mr. Smith." Mr. Smith says, "I understand that Judge Parmelee is to speak to us at the next meeting. Judge Parmelee is an able and distinguished speaker. It will be a great privilege to hear him. Since he is a very busy man, I believe we should make his talk the special order for that day so that he may address us just as soon as he arrives no matter what other business may be pending at that time." If this motion is seconded and carried by a two-thirds vote, then Judge Parmelee's talk is the special order for the next meeting and the chairman is ordered to present him to the assembly just as soon as he arrives regardless of what other business is pending at that time.

General or special orders may be created by the Constitution or By-Laws. Thus many Constitutions (or By-Laws) provide that "the annual election of officers shall be held the first meeting in September," (a general order). Or "the election of officers for the new year shall be held immediately after the reading of the minutes at the September meeting", (a special order). Such an order being a "constitutional order" can be changed, of course, only by suspending or amending the Constitution. "Orders," whether general, special or constitutional are called "Orders of the Day" for the meeting to which they apply.

The secretary should have a list of the orders of the day, if there be any, ready for the chairman to use in announcing to the assembly the order of business for that meeting. If the chairman fails to present to the assembly some item of business that is an order of the day for that meeting, a member may remind him by rising and without waiting to be recognized calling out, "Mr. Chairman, I call for the orders of the day!" (See page 4 in manual.)

Committees that are to report at this meeting should be listed on the memorandum sheet much the same as special and general orders so that none will be forgotten.

Committee Reports
    Social Committee—Year's Program
    Finance Committee—Budget

Abbreviations, symbols and diagrams are of great value in recording events quickly. For instance: "Have picnic. J. Brown" is all that is necessary to record that "J. Brown moved that the Lincoln Athletic Club give a nice picnic somewhere. This was seconded." If the secretary has already written down a motion which was declared out of order or lost for want of a second this should be noted as follows:—

Have picnic—J. Brown. $\left\{ \begin{array}{l} \text{lost, no second,} \\ \text{or, out of order.} \end{array} \right.$

Plenty of space should be left below each main motion so that all subsidiary, incidental and privileged motions moved may be shown in their proper relation to this main motion. The following will illustrate:—

Have picnic—J. Brown.
        at Sunset Park
        Lay on Table (better still, just "Table").

or Have dance—H. Smith.
            at Trilby Hall
            at 8:30 Saturday night
        Refer to Social Com.
        Close Debate
    Table

Adjourn

The motion to adjourn is not attached to the main motion because it does not apply to the main motion. It applies to the assembly. The motion to close debate is attached to the motion to refer because it applied to debate on the motion to refer and not to debate on the amendment or on the main motion. The motions to table, to refer and both amendments are attached to the main motion, because each of these subsidiary motions did apply to the main motion. When in doubt as to what motion may be applied to what other motion the secretary may find out instantly by looking at item one or item eight in the chart under each motion in the manual.

When the main motion has been disposed of in some manner so that there is no pending motion before the assembly it is worthwhile to make this clear by marking a line clear across the page like this:—

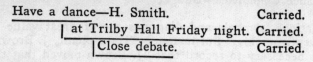

Have a dance—H. Smith.   Carried.
| at Trilby Hall Friday night. Carried.
|Close debate.   Carried.

Have a card party—
| Friday night, Nov. 14.
Refer to Social Com.   Carried.

The illustration below will show how a more complete record may be kept with the minimum of writing by the use of the diagram together with a reference letter for each motion and the addition of two words to the action taken.

a----Have a dance—J. Brown---------- carried after c.
b---- | at Trilby Hall ------ carried when moved.
c---- | at 8:30 Sat. night ------ carried after h.
d----   refer to Soc. Com. ------ lost after e.
e---- | close debate ------ carried after f.
f----   Table ------ lost
g----   Adjourn ------ lost
h----   close debate all ------ carried after d.

The order in which the motions come in the diagram shows the order in which they were moved. In case a motion applies to a motion not immediately above it, this may be indicated by connecting it directly to the motion to which it applies with a half circle to show where this connecting line crosses the line of motions to which it does not apply. If more than one motion is pending when the motion to close debate on all pending questions is carried, this motion to close debate should be attached to the motion immediately pending. The word "all" after the motion to close debate makes it clear that it does apply to all pending questions.

FINAL MINUTES OF MEETING OF JAN. 10, 1932

The regular monthly meeting of the Lincoln Athletic Club was called to order by the President, John Tremain, Monday, January 10, 1932 at 2:00 o'clock in the gymnasium. The minutes of the previous meeting were read and approved. A motion by J. Brown to raise the dues from 25 to 50 cents a month beginning with the month of March, 1932 was carried. A motion by H. Smith for the Athletic Committee to arrange with Garfield School for a track-meet was also carried. The motion by Mary Jenkins to donate $25 to the school charity fund was tabled. A motion by Harry Jones to have a dance was postponed till the next meeting. The report of the Social Committee on the Year's Activity Calendar was unanimously accepted. The treasurer's report for the year 1931 was received and placed on file (see footnote below). Having no further business the meeting was adjourned.

Respectfully submitted,

Mary Jane Brown,
Secretary.

John Tremain,
    President.

Footnote:—The treasurer's report should not be accepted until it has been carefully examined by an auditing committee and checked against the receipts, cancelled checks, cash on hand, etc. The treasurer's report is "received and placed on file" for the auditing committee. The report of the auditing committee is "accepted" or "rejected."

Note:—A very good collection of model minutes, committee reports and other forms used by organizations will be found in the appendix to "Textbook on Parliamentary Law" by Hall and Sturgis, published by Macmillan, 1930.

NOTES FOR MEETING FEB. 7, 1932.

Preliminary Memorandum for Chairman

1. Call meeting to order.

2. Reading and approval of Minutes.

3. Orders of Day,
   a. Special Orders,
      None.
   b. General Orders,
      Have dance—Postponed from Jan. 10.

4. Unfinished Business—None.

5. Committee Reports.
   a. Athletic Com.—On Garfield Sch. track meet.
      Finance Com.—On Budget for 1932.

6. New Business,
   In order here "to take from table motion to donate $25.00 to School Charity Fund" tabled Jan. 10.

1. Called to order by Jack Tremain, Pres. 2:15 P. M.

2. Minutes approved as corrected.
   Correction—Motion to raise dues moved by Fred Johnson instead of J. Brown.

3. a.____Have a dance _____ Carried after e.
   b.____ | at Trilby Hall _____ Carried after c.
   c.____ | Refer to Soc. Com. _____ Lost after d.
   d.____ | Close Debate _____ Carried
   e.____ | March 19, at 8:30 _____ Carried after f.
   f.____ | Table _____ Lost.

4. None.

5. Athletic Com. Report
   Lincoln-Garfield Track Meet July 1, approved.
   Finance Com. Report.
   Proposed Budget for 1932 referred back to Com.

6. a.____Take from table____Carried.
   b.__Donate $25.00 to School Charity Fund. Cd. after e.
   c.__ | in weekly payments of $5.00 Cd. after d.
   d.__ | close debate Cd.
   e.__ | beginning March 1 Cd. after c.

---

   a.___Have orchestra. John Graham. Lost after f.
   b.___ | Postp. to next meeting Lost after d.
   c.___ | Refer to Music | Com. Out of order, b pending.
   d.__ | Close debate | Lost after e.
   e.__ | Table Lost.
   f.__ | Adjourn Lost after b.

---

a.____Moved—Audit committee of three be appointed by Chair to audit Treasurer's accounts. Mary Powers. Carried after b.
b.____ | Strike out 3, insert 5 Lost.

Chair appointed Harvey Benson, Mary Powers and Fred Goldman.

Adjourn—Carried 3:10 P. M.

M. J. B.

The regular monthly meeting of the Lincoln Athletic Club was called to order by the President, John Tremain, Monday, Feb. 7 at 2:15 in the gymnasium. The minutes of the previous meeting were read and approved as corrected.

The motion to have a dance, postponed at the January meeting, was carried after being amended to read that we have a dance at Trilby Hall March 19 at 8:30.

The Athletic Committee reported that arrangements had been made with Garfield School for a Track Meet July first. This was approved.

The Finance Committee presented the budget for the year 1932. This was referred back to the committee for further consideration.

The motion to donate $25.00 to the school Charity Fund was taken from the table and carried after being amended to read that we donate $25.00 to the school Charity Fund in weekly payments of $5.00 beginning March 1.

A motion to have an orchestra was moved by John Graham, seconded and lost.

It was moved by Mary Powers, seconded and carried that an Audit Committee of three be appointed by the Chair to audit the treasurer's accounts. The Chair appointed Harvey Benson, Mary Powers, and Fred Goldman for this committee.

The meeting adjourned on motion at 3:10 P. M.

Mary Jane Brown,
Secretary.

John Tremain,
President.

DUTIES OF A SECRETARY

1. To keep a careful and authentic record of the proceedings of the organization.

2. To prepare a roll call of members and call it when necessary.

3. To call the meeting to order in the absence of the presiding officer.

4. To preserve all documents of the organization except those specifically assigned to others.

5. To provide the chairman of each committee with a list

of the members of his committee together with all the papers and instructions intended for it.

6. To provide the presiding officer at the beginning of each meeting with the order of business for that day.

7. To read all the papers that may be called for by the assembly.

8. To authenticate by his signature all records, documents, etc.

9. To bring to each meeting a copy of the constitution, by-laws, and the standing rules of the organization, together with a list of the members of all standing and special committees.

10. To carry on all official correspondence for the organization.

a. When this duty involves much work it is frequently assigned to a correspondence secretary.

This manual and these lessons are designed to cover only the minimum essentials of parliamentary procedure. For a more complete discussion of motions, duties of officers, committees and committee reports consult the standard texts. such as Robert's "Rules of Order," the "House Rules and Manual" (Congressional Manual), "Legislative Procedure" by Robert Luce, etc.

(1)